Fodor's 93
Pocket
San Francisco

D1026528

Reprinted from *Fodor's San Francisco '93*

Fodor's Travel Publications, Inc.
New York • Toronto • London •
Sydney • Auckland

Fodor's Pocket San Francisco

Editors: Denise L. Nolty, Larry Peterson
Contributors: John Burks, Toni Chapman, Lau-
ra Del Rosso, Pamela Faust, Sheila Gadsden,
Jacqueline Killeen, Marcy Pritchard, Linda K.
Schmidt, Aaron Shurin, Dan Spitzer, Robert
Taylor, Casey Tefertiller
Creative Director: Fabrizio La Rocca
Cartographer: David Lindroth
Illustrator: Karl Tanner
Cover Photograph: Stephenson/Westlight
Design: Vignelli Associates

Special Sales

Fodor's Travel Publications are available at special discounts for bulk purchases (100 copies or
more) for sales promotions or premiums. Special
editions can be created in large quantities for
special needs. For more information write to
Special Marketing, Fodor's Travel Publications,
201 East 50th St., New York, NY 10022; Ran-
dom House of Canada, Ltd., Marketing Dept.,
1265 Aerowood Dr., Mississauga, Ont. L4W
1B9; or Fodor's Travel Publications, 20 Vauxhall
Bridge Rd., London, England SW1V 2SA.
MANUFACTURED IN THE UNITED STATES OF
AMERICA
10 9 8 7 6 5 4 3 2 1

Contents

Maps

Foreword

While every care has been taken to assure the accuracy of the information in this guide, the passage of time will always bring change and, consequently, the publisher cannot accept responsibility for errors that may occur.

All prices and opening times quoted here are based on information supplied to us at press time. Hours and admission fees may change, however, and the prudent traveler will avoid inconvenience by calling ahead.

Fodor's wants to hear about your travel experiences, both pleasant and unpleasant. When a hotel or restaurant fails to live up to its billing, let us know and we will investigate the complaint and revise our entries where the facts warrant it.

Send your letters to the editors of Fodor's Travel Publications, 201 E. 50th Street, New York, NY 10022.

San Francisco

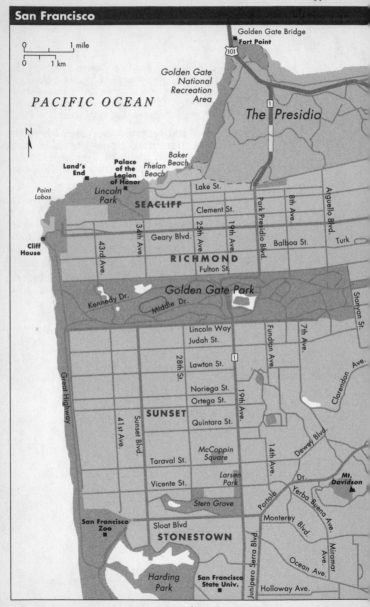

0 ___ 1 mile
0 ___ 1 km

PACIFIC OCEAN

N

Golden Gate Bridge
Fort Point

101

Golden Gate
National
Recreation
Area

The Presidia

1

Land's
End

Palace
of the
Legion
of Honor

Phelan
Beach

Baker
Beach

Point
Lobos

Lincoln
Park

Lake St.

SEACLIFF

Clement St.

Park Presidio Blvd.

8th Ave.

Arguello Blvd.

Cliff
House

43rd Ave.

34th Ave.

Geary Blvd.

25th Ave.

19th Ave.

Balboa St.

Turk

RICHMOND

Fulton St.

Golden Gate Park

Kennedy Dr.

Middle Dr.

Stanyan St.

Lincoln Way
Judah St.

Funston Ave.

7th Ave.

Great Highway

28th St.

Lawton St.

1

Clarendon Ave.

Noriega St.
Ortega St.

41st Ave.

Sunset Blvd.

SUNSET

Quintara St.

19th Ave.

14th Ave.

Dewey Blvd.

Taraval St.

McCoppin
Square

Vicente St.

Larsen
Park

Dr.

Mt.
Davidson

Stern Grove

Portola

Yerba Buena Ave.

San Francisco
Zoo

Sloat Blvd

Monterey
Blvd.

Miramar
Ave.

STONESTOWN

Juniper Serra Blvd.

Ocean Ave.

Harding
Park

San Francisco
State Univ.

Holloway Ave.

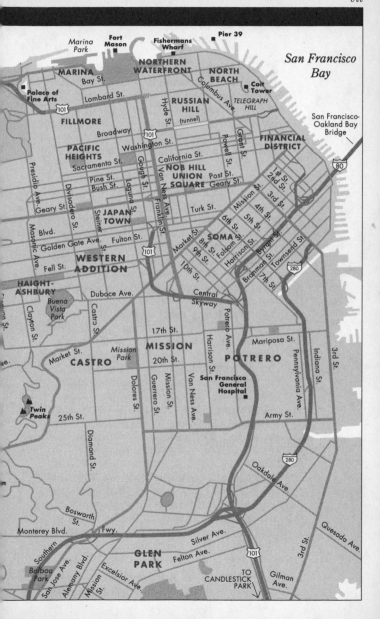

San Francisco Bay

Marina Park
Fort Mason
Fishermans Wharf
Pier 39
Palace of Fine Arts
MARINA
Bay St.
NORTHERN WATERFRONT
NORTH BEACH
Colt Tower
TELEGRAPH HILL
Lombard St.
Hyde St.
Columbus Ave.
RUSSIAN HILL
(tunnel)
San Francisco-Oakland Bay Bridge
FILLMORE
Broadway
Washington St.
Grant St.
Powell St.
FINANCIAL DISTRICT
PACIFIC HEIGHTS
Sacramento St.
California St.
NOB HILL
UNION SQUARE
Post St.
1st St.
2nd St.
3rd St.
Pine St.
Bush St.
Gough St.
Van Ness Ave.
Geary St.
Mission St.
4th St.
5th St.
6th St.
Presidio Ave.
Divisadero St.
Laguna St.
Franklin St.
JAPAN TOWN
Steiner St.
Turk St.
Market St.
7th St.
8th St.
Folsom St.
Harrison St.
Bryant St.
Townsend St.
Geary St.
Masonic Ave.
Blvd.
Golden Gate Ave.
Fulton St.
SOMA
9th St.
Branman St.
Fell St.
WESTERN ADDITION
10th St.
HAIGHT-ASHBURY
Clayton St.
Buena Vista Park
Dubace Ave.
Castro St.
Central Skyway
Potrero Ave.
CASTRO
Market St.
Mission Park
17th St.
MISSION
20th St.
Harrison St.
Mission St.
Van Ness Ave.
POTRERO
Mariposa St.
Pennsylvania Ave.
Indiana St.
3rd St.
Twin Peaks
Diamond St.
25th St.
Dolores St.
Guerrero St.
San Francisco General Hospital
Army St.
Bosworth St.
Fwy.
Monterey Blvd.
Oakdale Ave.
Quesada Ave.
Southern
Balboa Park
San Jose Ave.
Alemany Blvd.
Mission St.
Excelsior Ave.
GLEN PARK
Silver Ave.
Felton Ave.
TO CANDLESTICK PARK
Gilman Ave.
3rd St.

Introduction

San Franciscans tend to regard the envy of visitors as a matter of course and to look on whatever brought them to settle here (there's probably never been a time when the majority of the population was native born) as a brilliant stroke of luck. Certain local problems can be traced to this warm contentment with the city and to the attendant fear that somebody might do something to *change* it. The skyline, for example, which in recent decades has become clotted with high rises, has turned into a source of controversy. The city's Financial District is dominated by the dark, looming Bank of America—the sculpted lump of black granite out front has been nicknamed "The Banker's Heart"—and by the Transamerica Building, the glass-and-concrete pyramid that has made the city's skyline instantly recognizable. (Nearly two decades after its construction, San Franciscans still argue vehemently about its merits, or its utter lack of them. But nobody claims it isn't distinctive.) Admirers of the skyline defend the skyscrapers as evidence of prosperity and of San Francisco's world-class stature; detractors grumble about the "Manhattanization" that's ruining a unique place. Historically, San Francisco is a boomtown, and various periods of frantic building have lined the pockets of developers for whom the city's beauty was no consideration at all. Nevertheless, in 1986 the voters set limits on downtown construction; now the controversy has moved out to the neighborhoods, where entrepreneurs want to knock down single-family houses to make room for profitable apartment buildings.

The boom began in 1848. At the beginning of that year, San Francisco wasn't much more than a pleasant little settlement that had been founded by the Spaniards back in the auspicious year of 1776. The natural harbor of the bay (so commodious that "all the navies of the world might fit" inside it, as one visitor wrote) made it a village with a future. The future came abruptly when gold was discovered at John Sutter's sawmill in the Sierra foothills, some 115 miles to the northeast. By 1850, San Francisco's population had zoomed from 500 to 30,000, and a "western Wall Street" sprang up as millions upon millions of dollars' worth of gold was panned and blasted out of the hills. The gold mines began to dry up in a few years; but in 1859 prospectors turned up a fabulously rich vein of silver in the Virginia Range, in what is now Nevada; and San Francisco—the nearest financial center—prospered again.

Not so many centuries ago the area that was to become San Francisco was a windswept, virtually treeless, and, above all, sandy wasteland. Sand even covered the hills. The sand is still there, but—except along the ocean—it's well hidden. City Hall is built on 80 feet of it. The westerly section of the city—the Sunset and Richmond districts and Golden Gate Park—seems flat only because sand has filled in the contours of the hills.

But the hills that remain are spectacular. They provide vistas all over the city—nothing is more common than to find yourself staring out toward Angel Island or Alcatraz, or across the bay at Berkeley and Oakland. The hills are also exceptionally good at winding pedestrians. (The cable cars didn't become instantly popular because they were picturesque.) The city's two bridges, which are almost as majestic as their surroundings, had their 50th birthdays in 1986 and 1987. The Golden Gate Bridge, which crosses to Marin County, got a bigger party, but the San

Francisco–Oakland Bay Bridge got a better present: a necklace of lights along its spans. They were supposed to be temporary, but the locals were so taken with the glimmer that bridge boosters started a drive to make them permanent; radio DJs and newspaper columnists put out daily appeals, drivers gave extra quarters to the toll takers, various corporations put up shares, and—close to a million dollars later—the lights on the Bay Bridge now shine nightly.

The city has three trademarks: the fog, the cable cars, and the Victorians. Bay-windowed, ornately decorated Victorian houses—the multicolor, ahistorical paint jobs that have become popular make them seem even more ornate—are the city's most distinguishing architectural feature. They date mainly from the latter part of Queen Victoria's reign, 1870 to the turn of the century. In those three decades, San Francisco more than doubled in population (from 150,000 to 342,000); the transcontinental railway, linking the once-isolated western capital to the east, had been completed in 1869. That may explain the exuberant confidence of the architecture.

In terms of both geography and culture, San Francisco is about as close as you can get to Asia in the continental United States. (The city prides itself on its role as a Pacific Rim capital, and overseas investment has become a vital part of its financial life.) The first great wave of Chinese immigrants came during the Gold Rush in 1852. Chinese workers quickly became the target of race hatred and discriminatory laws; Chinatown—which began when the Chinese moved into old buildings that white businesses seeking more fashionable locations had abandoned—developed, as much as anything else, as a refuge. Chinatown is still a fascinating place to wander, and it's a good bet for late-night food, but it's not the whole story by any means. The Asian community, which now accounts for a fifth of San Francisco's population, reaches into every San Francisco neighborhood, and particularly into the Sunset and Richmond districts, out toward the ocean. Clement Street, which runs through the center of Richmond, has become the main thoroughfare of a second Chinatown. Southeast Asian immigrants, many of them ethnic Chinese, are transforming the seedy Tenderloin into a thriving Little Indochina. There was heavy Japanese immigration earlier in this century, but most of it went to southern California, where organized labor had less of a foothold and where there were greater opportunities for Asian workers. Still, San Francisco has its Japantown, with its massive Japan Center complex and scads of shops and restaurants clustered in and around it. In the past, Asians have tended toward a backseat—or at least an offstage—role in the city's politics; but like so much else on the city's cultural/political landscape, that, too, seems to be changing.

San Francisco has always been a loose, tolerant—some would say licentious—city. As early as the 1860s, the "Barbary Coast" —a collection of taverns, whorehouses, and gambling joints along Pacific Avenue close to the waterfront—was famous, or infamous. Bohemian communities seem to thrive here. In the 1950s, North Beach, the city's Little Italy, became the home of the Beat Movement. (Herb Caen, the city's best-known columnist, coined the term "beatnik.") Lawrence Ferlinghetti's City Lights, a bookstore and publishing house that brought out, among other titles, Allen Ginsberg's *Howl* and *Kaddish*, still stands on Columbus Avenue as a monument to the era. (Across Broadway, a plaque identifies the Condor as the site of the nation's first topless and bottomless performances, a monument to a slightly later era.) The Bay Area was the epicenter of '60s ferment, too. The Free Speech Movement began at the University of California in Berkeley (where, in October 1965, Allen Ginsberg introduced the term "flower power"). The Haight-Ashbury district was synonymous with hippiedom.

Southwest of the Haight is the onetime Irish neighborhood known as the Castro, which during the 1970s became identified with lesbian and gay liberation. Castro Street is dominated by the elaborate Castro Theatre, a 1923 vision in Spanish Baroque, which presents one of the best repertory movie schedules in the city. (The grand old pipe organ still plays during intermissions, breaking into "San Francisco" just before the feature begins.) There's been much talk, most of it exaggerated, about how AIDS has chastened and "matured" the Castro; it's still an effervescent neighborhood, and—as housing everywhere has become more and more of a prize—an increasingly mixed one. At the same time, gays, like Asians, are moving out of the ghetto and into neighborhoods all around the city.

The mix of ethnic, economic, social, and sexual groups can be bewildering, but the city's residents—whatever their origin—face it with aplomb and even gratitude. Everybody in San Francisco has an opinion about where to get the best burrito or the hottest Szechuan eggplant or the strongest cappuccino. The most staid citizens have learned how to appreciate good camp. Nearly everyone smiles on the fortunate day they arrived on, or were born on, this windy, foggy patch of peninsula.

1 Essential Information

Before You Go

Visitor Information

For general information and free booklets and maps, contact the **San Francisco Convention and Visitors Bureau** (201 3rd St., Suite 900, 94103, tel. 415/974-6900). The bureau also publishes an attractive 80-page guide, *The San Francisco Book*, in three editions a year; it includes up-to-date information on theater offerings, art exhibits, sporting events, and other special happenings. Send $1 for postage and handling to SFCVB, Box 6977, 94101. In San Francisco, stop by the **Visitor's Information Center** (tel. 415/391-2000) in Hallidie Plaza's lower level, at Powell and Market streets. The office is open Monday through Friday 9-5:30, Saturday 9-3, and Sunday 10-2.

The **Redwood Empire Association Visitor Information Center** (785 Market St., 15th floor, 94103, 415/543-8334) will provide a wealth of free information on San Francisco and surrounding areas, including the wine country, the redwood groves, and northwestern California. For a dollar postage they will also send *The Redwood Empire Visitor's Guide*.

The San Francisco Bay Area encompasses dozens of towns, and many of them have chambers of commerce that are happy to provide travelers with information. Here are the addresses of a few of the largest:

Berkeley Chamber of Commerce (1834 University Ave., Box 210, Berkeley, CA 94703, tel. 510/549-7003).
Oakland Convention and Visitors Bureau (1000 Broadway, Suite 200, Oakland, CA 94607, tel. 510/839-9000 or 800/262-5526).
San Jose Convention and Visitors Bureau (333 W. San Carlos St., Suite 1000, San Jose, CA 95110, tel. 408/295-9600).

A detailed 208-page book, *Discover the Californias*, which includes an informative section on the Bay Area, is available free through the **California Office of Tourism** (tel. 800/862-2543). In addition, the California Office of Tourism (801 K

St., Suite 1600, Sacramento, CA 95814, tel. 916/
322–1397) can answer many questions about
travel in the state.

Tips for British Travelers

Passports You will need a valid 10-year passport (cost £15).
and Visas You do not need a visa if you are staying for 90
days or less, have a return ticket, or are flying
with a participating airline, and complete a Visa
Waiver Form I–94W, available at the airport or
on the plane. There are some exceptions to this,
so check with your travel agent or with the
United States Embassy (Visa and Immigration
Dept., 5 Upper Grosvenor St., London W1A
2JB, tel. 071/499–3443). No vaccinations are required.

Customs Visitors 21 or over can take in (1) 200 cigarettes
or 50 cigars or 2 kilograms of smoking tobacco,
(2) 1 liter of alcohol, and (3) duty-free gifts to a
value of $100. Do not try to take in meat or meat
products, seeds, plants, or fruits. Avoid illegal
drugs like the plague.

Returning to the United Kingdom, you may take
home (1) 200 cigarettes or 100 cigarillos or 50
cigars or 250 grams of tobacco; (2) 2 liters of
table wine and (a) 1 liter of alcohol over 22% by
volume (most spirits) or (b) 2 liters of alcohol
under 22% by volume (fortified or sparkling
wine) or (c) 2 more liters of table wine; (3) 60
milliliters of perfume and 250 milliliters of
toilet water; and (4) other goods up to a value
of £32 but not more than 50 liters of beer or 25
lighters.

Insurance We recommend that you insure yourself against
sickness and motoring mishaps with **Europ
Assistance** (252 High St., Croydon, Surrey CR0
1NF, tel. 081/680–1234). It is also wise to take
out insurance to cover loss of luggage (though
check to see whether or not you are already covered through your existing homeowner's policy). Trip-cancellation insurance is another wise
buy. The **Association of British Insurers** (51
Gresham St., LondonEC2V 7HQ, tel. 071/600–
3333) will give comprehensive advice on all as-
pects of vacation insurance.

Tour Operators As a result of the price battle that has raged over transatlantic fares, most tour operators now offer excellent budget packages to the United States. Among those you might consider as you plan your trip are:

British Airways Holidays (Atlantic House, Hazelwick Ave., Three Bridges, Crawley, West Sussex RH10 1NP, tel. 0293/611611).

Cosmosair plc (Ground Floor, Dale House, Tiviot Dale, Stockport, Cheshire SK1 1TB, tel. 061/480–5799).

Jetsave (Sussex House, London Rd., East Grinstead, West Sussex RH19 1LD, tel. 0342/312033).

Key to America (15 Feltham Rd., Ashford, Middlesex TW15 1DQ, tel. 0784/248777).

Kuoni Travel Ltd. (Kuoni House, Dorking, Surrey RH5 4AZ, tel. 0306/76711).

Premier Holidays (Premier Travel Center, Westbrook, Milton Rd., Cambridge CB4, 1YQ, tel. 0223/355977).

Airfares Many ticket brokers offer budget flights to San Francisco. Some of these fares can be extremely difficult to come by, however, so be sure to book well in advance. Also check on APEX and other money-saving fares through the airlines or your travel agent. The small ads of daily and Sunday newspapers are another good source of information on low-cost flights.

When to Go

Any time of the year is the right time to go to San Francisco, acknowledged to be one of the most beautiful cities in the world. The city itself enjoys a temperate marine climate. The fog rolls in during the summer, but it seems less an inconvenience than part of the atmosphere of this never-mundane place. As long as you remember to bring along sweaters and jackets, even in August, you can't miss.

San Francisco is on the tip of a peninsula, surrounded on three sides by the Pacific Ocean and San Francisco Bay. Its climate is quintessentially marine and moderate: It never gets very hot—anything above 80 degrees is reported as a shocking heat wave—or very cold (as far as the thermometer is concerned, anyway).

For all its moderation, however, San Francisco can be tricky. In the summertime, fog often rolls in from the ocean, blocking the sun and filling the air with dampness. At times like this you'll want a coat, jacket, or warm sweater instead of the shorts or lightweight summer clothes that seem so comfortable in most North American cities during July and August. Mark Twain is credited with observing that the coldest winter he ever spent was one summer in San Francisco. He may have been exaggerating, but it's best not to expect a hot summer in this city.

If you travel to the north, east, or south of the city, you will find the summer months much warmer. Shirtsleeves and thin cottons are usually just fine for the Wine Country.

Be prepared for some rain during the winter months, especially December and January. Winds off the ocean can add to the chill factor, so pack some warm clothing to be on the safe side.

Climate The following are average daily maximum and minimum temperatures for San Francisco.

Jan.	55F	13C	May	66F	19C	Sept.	73F	23C
	41	5		48	9		51	11
Feb.	59F	15C	June	69F	21C	Oct.	69F	21C
	42	6		51	11		50	10
Mar.	60F	16C	July	69F	21C	Nov.	64F	18C
	44	7		51	11		44	7
Apr.	62F	17C	Aug.	69F	21C	Dec.	57F	14C
	46	8		53	12		42	6

Current weather information on more than 750 cities around the world—450 of them in the United States—is only a phone call away. Dialing **WeatherTrak** at 900/370-8728 will connect you with a computer, with which you can communicate by touch tone—at a cost of 95¢ per minute. The number plays a taped message that tells you to dial a three-digit code for the destination in which you are interested. The code is either the area code (in the United States) or the first three letters of the foreign city. For a list of all access codes, send a stamped, self-addressed envelope to Cities, 98 Terrace Way, Greensboro, NC 27403. For further information, call 800/247-3282.

What to Pack

Clothing The most important single rule to bear in mind
when packing for a vacation in the San Francisco Bay Area is to prepare for changes in temperature. An hour's drive can take you up or down
many degrees, and the variation from daytime
to nighttime in a single location is often marked.
Take along sweaters, jackets, and clothes for
layering as your best insurance for coping with
variations in temperature. Include shorts and/
or cool cottons unless you are packing only for a
midwinter ski trip. Always tuck in a bathing
suit. You may not be a beach lover, but the majority of overnight lodgings include a pool, a spa,
and a sauna; you'll want the option of using these
facilities.

Although casual dressing is a hallmark of the
California lifestyle, men will need a jacket and
tie for many good restaurants in the evening,
and women will be more comfortable in something dressier than regulation sightseeing garb.

Considerations of formality aside, bear in mind
that San Francisco can be chilly at any time of
the year, especially in summer, when the fog is
apt to descend and stay. Nothing is more pitiful
than the sight of uninformed tourists in shorts,
their legs blue with cold. Take along clothes that
will keep you warm, even if the season doesn't
seem to warrant it.

Miscellaneous Although you can buy supplies of film, sunburn
cream, aspirin, and most other necessities almost anywhere in California (unless you're
heading for the wilderness), it is a bother, especially if your time is limited, to have to search for
staples. Take along a reasonable supply of the
things you know you will be using routinely, and
save your time for sheer enjoyment.

An extra pair of glasses, contact lenses, or prescription sunglasses is always a good idea; the
loss of your only pair can damage a vacation.

It is important to pack any prescription medications you need regularly as well as prescriptions
that are occasionally important, such as allergy
medications. If you know you are prone to certain medical problems and have good, simple

ways of dealing with early manifestations, take
along what you might need, even though you
may never use it.

Arriving and Departing

By Plane

San Francisco International Airport is just
south of the city, off U.S. 101. American carri-
ers serving San Francisco are **Alaska Air, Amer-
ican, Continental, Delta, Southwest, TWA,
United,** and **USAir.** International carriers in-
clude **Air Canada, Canadian Pacific, Japan Air
Lines, British Airways, China Airlines, Qantas,
Air New Zealand, Mexicana,** and **Lufthansa.**
Many of these same airlines serve the Oakland
Airport, which is across the bay but not much
farther away from downtown San Francisco (via
I-880 and I-80), although traffic on the Bay
Bridge may at times make travel time longer.

When booking reservations, keep in mind the
distinction between nonstop flights (no stops
and no changes), direct flights (no changes of
aircraft, but one or more stops), and connecting
flights (one or more changes of planes at one or
more stops). Connecting flights are often the
least expensive, but they are the most time-con-
suming and the biggest nuisance.

Smoking Smoking is banned on all scheduled routes within the 48 contiguous states; within the states of
Hawaii and Alaska; to and from the U.S. Virgin
Islands and Puerto Rico; and on flights of under
six hours to and from Hawaii and Alaska. The
rule applies to the domestic legs of all foreign
routes but does not affect international flights.

On a flight where smoking is permitted, you can
request a nonsmoking seat during check-in or
when you book your ticket. If the airline tells
you there are no seats available in the
nonsmoking section on the day of the flight, in-
sist on one: Department of Transportation regulations require U.S. carriers to find seats for
all nonsmokers, provided they meet check-in
time restrictions.

Luggage
Regulations
Carry-on
Luggage
Passengers aboard major U.S. carriers are usually limited to two carry-on bags. For a bag you wish to store under the seat, the maximum dimensions are 9″ × 14″ × 22″. For bags that can be hung in a closet or on a luggage rack, the maximum dimensions are 4″ × 23″ × 45″. For bags you wish to store in an overhead bin, the maximum dimensions are 10″ × 14″ × 36″. Your two carryons must each fit one of these sets of dimensions, and any item that exceeds the specified dimensions is generally rejected as a carryon and handled as checked baggage. Keep in mind that an airline can adapt these rules to circumstances; don't be surprised when you are allowed only one carry-on bag on an especially crowded flight.

The rules list eight items that may be carried aboard in addition to the two carryons: a handbag (pocketbook or purse), an overcoat or wrap, an umbrella, a camera, a reasonable amount of reading material, an infant bag, and crutches, a cane, braces, or other prosthetic device upon which the passenger is dependent. Infant/child safety seats can also be brought aboard if parents have purchased a ticket for the child or if there is space in the cabin.

Note that these regulations are for U.S. airlines only. Foreign airlines generally allow one piece of carry-on luggage in tourist class, in addition to handbags and bags filled with duty-free goods. Passengers in first and business classes are also allowed to carry on one garment bag. It is best to check with your airline in advance to confirm its rules regarding carry-on luggage.

Checked
Luggage
U.S. airlines allow passengers to check two or three suitcases whose total dimensions (length + width + height) do not exceed 62″ and whose weight does not exceed 70 pounds.

Rules governing foreign airlines vary from one airline to another, so check with your travel agent or the airline itself before you go. All airlines allow passengers to check two bags. In general, expect the weight restriction on the two bags to be not more than 70 pounds each, and the size restriction to be 62″ total dimensions for each bag.

Lost Luggage   Airlines are responsible for lo
property only up to $1,250 per pa
mestic flights; $9.07 per pound (
for checked baggage on interna
and up to $400 per passenger for u_____ bag-
gage on international flights. When you carry
valuables, either take them with you on the airplane or purchase additional insurance for lost
luggage. Some airlines will issue additional luggage insurance when you check in, but many do
not. One that does is American Airlines. Rates
for domestic and international flights are $2 for
every $100 valuation, with a maximum of $5,000
valuation per passenger. Hand luggage is not included.

Insurance for lost, damaged, or stolen luggage
is available through travel agents or from various insurance companies. Two that issue luggage insurance are Tele-Trip, a subsidiary of
Mutual of Omaha, and The Travelers.

Tele-Trip (tel. 800/228–9792) operates sales
booths at airports and issues insurance through
travel agents. Tele-Trip will insure checked luggage for up to 180 days; rates vary according to
the length of the trip.

The Travelers (Ticket and Travel Dept., 1 Tower
Sq., Hartford, CT 06183–5040, tel. 203/277–
0111 or 800/243–3174) will insure checked or
hand luggage for $500 to $2,000 valuation per
person, for a maximum of 180 days. For 1 to 5
days, the rate for a $500 valuation is $10; for 180
days, $85. The two companies offer the same
rates on both domestic and international flights.
Consult the travel pages of your Sunday newspaper for the names of other companies that insure luggage. Before you travel, itemize the
contents of each bag in case you need to file an
insurance claim. Be certain to put your home ad-
dress on each piece of luggage, including carry-
on bags. If your luggage is stolen and later re-
covered, the airline will deliver the luggage to
your home free of charge.

From the   **SFO Airporter** (tel. 415/495–8404) provides bus
Airport to   service between downtown and the airport,
Downtown   making the round of downtown hotels. Buses
run every 20 minutes from 5 AM to 11 PM, from

the lower level outside the baggage claim area. The fare is $7 one-way, $11 round-trip.

For $11, **Supershuttle** will take you from the airport to anywhere within the city limits of San Francisco. At the airport, after picking up your luggage, call 415/871–7800 and a van will pick you up within five minutes. To go to the airport, make reservations (tel. 415/558–8500) 24 hours in advance. The Supershuttle stops at the upper level of the terminal, along with several other bus and van transport services.

Taxis to or from downtown take 20–30 minutes and average $30.

By Train

Amtrak (tel. 800/USA–RAIL) trains (the *Zephyr*, from Chicago via Denver, and the *Coast Starlight*, traveling between San Diego and Seattle) stop at the Oakland Depot; from there buses will take you across the Bay Bridge to the Transbay Terminal at 1st and Mission streets in San Francisco.

By Bus

Greyhound/Trailways serves San Francisco from the Transbay Terminal at 1st and Mission streets (tel. 415/558–6789).

By Car

Route I-80 finishes its westward journey from New York's George Washington Bridge at the Bay Bridge, linking Oakland and San Francisco. U.S. 101, running north–south through the entire state, enters the city across the Golden Gate Bridge and continues south down the peninsula, along the west side of the bay.

Staying in San Francisco

Important Addresses and Numbers

Tourist Information The **San Francisco Convention and Visitors Bureau** maintains a visitors information center on the lower level at Hallidie Plaza (Powell and Market streets), just three blocks from Union Square, near the cable car turnaround and the

Powell Street entrance to BART. *Weekdays 9–5, Sat. 9–3, Sun. 10–2. Tel. 415/974–6900. Summary of daily events: tel. 415/391–2001.*

Emergencies **Police** or **ambulance,** telephone 911.

Doctors Two hospitals with 24-hour emergency rooms are **San Francisco General Hospital** (1001 Potrero Ave., tel. 415/821–8200) and the **Medical Center at the University of California, San Francisco** (500 Parnassus Ave. at 3rd Ave., near Golden Gate Park, tel. 415/476–1000).

Access Health Care provides drop-in medical care at two San Francisco locations, daily 8–8. No membership is necessary. *In Davies Medical Center, Castro St. at Duboce Ave., tel. 415/565–6600; and 26 California St. at Drumm St., tel. 415/397–2881.*

Pharmacies Several **Walgreen Drug Stores** have 24-hour pharmacies, including stores at 500 Geary Street near Union Square (tel. 415/673–8413) and 3201 Divisadero Street at Lombard Street (tel. 415/931–6417). Also try the Walgreen pharmacy on Powell Street near Market Street. *135 Powell St., tel. 415/391–7222. Open Mon.–Sat. 8 AM–midnight, Sun. 9 AM–8 PM. AE, MC, V.*

Getting Around

Because San Francisco is relatively compact and because it's so very difficult to find parking, we recommend that you do your exploring on foot or by bus as much as possible. You may not need a car at all, except perhaps for exploring the Presidio, Golden Gate Park, Lincoln Park, the Western Shoreline, and for making excursions out of town.

How to Get There from Union Square is a handy free booklet that will tell you how to reach approximately 50 points of interest in the city by public transportation. You can pick it up at the Redwood Empire Association Visitor Information Center (785 Market St., 15th floor, tel. 415/543–8334) on weekdays 9 AM–4:30 AM.

By BART **Bay Area Rapid Transit** (tel. 415/788–BART) sends air-conditioned aluminum trains at speeds of up to 80 miles an hour across the bay to Oakland, Berkeley, Concord, Richmond, and

Fremont. Trains also travel south from San Francisco as far as Daly City. Wall maps in the stations list destinations and fares (85¢–$3). Trains run Mon.–Sat. 6 AM–midnight, Sun. 9 AM–midnight.

A $2.60 excursion ticket buys a three-county tour. You can visit any of the 34 stations for up to four hours as long as you exit and enter at the same station.

By Bus The **San Francisco Municipal Railway System,** or **Muni** (tel. 415/673–MUNI), includes buses and trolleys, surface streetcars, and the new below-surface streetcars, as well as cable cars. There is 24-hour service, and the fare is 85¢ for adults, 15¢ for senior citizens, and 25¢ for children ages 5–17. Exact change is always required. Free transfers are available.

A $6 pass good for unlimited travel all day ($10 for three days) on all routes can be purchased from ticket machines at cable car terminals and at the Visitor Information Center in Hallidie Plaza (Powell and Market Sts.).

By Cable Car "They turn corners almost at right angles; cross other lines, and for all I know, may run up the sides of houses," wrote Rudyard Kipling in 1889. In 1984 the 109-year-old system returned to service after a $58.2 million overhaul. Because the cable cars had been declared a National Historic Landmark in 1964, renovation methods and materials had to preserve the historical and traditional qualities of Andrew Hallidie's system. The rehabilitated moving landmark has been designed to withstand another century of use.

The Powell-Mason line (No. 59) and the Powell-Hyde line (No. 60) begin at Powell and Market streets near Union Square and terminate at Fisherman's Wharf. The California Street line (No. 61) runs east and west from Market Street near the Embarcadero to Van Ness Avenue.

Cable cars are popular, crowded, and an experience to ride: Move toward one quickly as it pauses, wedge yourself into any available space, and hold on! The views from many cars are spectacular, and the sensation of moving up and down some of San Francisco's steepest hills in a

small, open-air clanging c⟨
missed.

The fare is $2 for adults.
Exact change is required

By Taxi Rates are high in the city, a⟨⟩
are relatively short. It is almost impos⟨⟩
hail a passing cab, especially on weekends. Either phone or use the nearest hotel taxi stand to
grab a cab. See the Yellow Pages for numbers of
taxi companies.

By Car Driving in San Francisco can be a challenge,
what with the hills, the one-way streets, and the
traffic. Take it easy, remember to curb your
wheels when parking on hills, and use public
transportation whenever possible. On certain
streets, parking is forbidden during rush hours.
Look for the warning signs; illegally parked cars
are towed. This is a great city for walking and a
terrible city for parking. Downtown parking
lots are often full and always expensive. Finding
a spot in North Beach at night, for instance, may
be impossible.

Guided Tours

In selecting a tour, bear in mind that the size of
the vehicle will affect the character of the tour to
some degree. Smaller vans can go to spots
where the larger buses cannot maneuver or are
not permitted, such as the Marina and the Palace of Fine Arts. Drivers of vans are sometimes
more amenable to stopping for picture taking.

Unless specifically noted, the costs given for
guided tours do not include meals or refreshments.

Orientation Tours **Golden City Tours** offers 14-passenger vans for
their six-hour city tours, which include a drive
across the Golden Gate Bridge to Sausalito and a
1½-hour stopover at Fisherman's Wharf. Customers are picked up at all major airport hotels.
A shorter afternoon tour omits Sausalito. *Tel.
415/692–3044. Tours daily. Make reservations
the day before. Cost: $28. Afternoon tour
$18.50.*

Golden Gate Tours uses both vans and buses for
its 3½-hour city tour, offered mornings and afternoons. You can combine the tour with a bay

cruise. Customers are picked up at hotels and motels. Senior citizen and group rates are available. *Tel. 415/788–5775. Tours daily. Make reservations the day before. Cost: $20 adults, $10.50 children under 12, $18.50 senior citizens. Cruise combo: $26 adults, $15 children under 12, $24.50 senior citizens.*

Gray Line offers a variety of tours of the city, the Bay Area, and northern California. Their city tour, on buses or double-decker buses, lasts 3½ hours and departs from the Trans-Bay Terminal at 1st and Mission streets five to six times daily. Gray Line also picks up at centrally located hotels. *Tel. 415/558–9400. Tours daily. Make reservations the day before. Cost: $23.50 adults, $11.75 children.*

The Great Pacific Tour uses 13-passenger vans for its daily 3½-hour city tour. Bilingual guides may be requested. They pick up at major San Francisco hotels. Tours are available to Monterey, the Wine Country, and Muir Woods. *Tel. 415/626–4499. Tours daily. Make reservations the day before, or, possibly, the same day. Cost: $25 adults, $24 senior citizens, $20 children 5–11.*

Pier 39 Cable Car Company offers hour-long tours of Chinatown, North Beach, and the surrounding neighborhoods on motorized cable cars. Tours depart every 45 minutes daily from the entrance plaza at Pier 39. *Tel. 415/981–8030. Cost: $12 adults, $10 senior citizens, $6 children.*

San Francisco Scenic Route. Near Escapes (Box 193005, San Francisco 94119, tel. 415/386–8687) has produced an audio cassette with music and sound effects that will take you in your own car "where the tour buses can't go." It will guide you past Fisherman's Wharf, Chinatown, Golden Gate Park, Twin Peaks, Ghirardelli Square, Mission Dolores, the Civic Center, and other tourist attractions. Another cassette offers a detailed walking tour of Chinatown; both come with route maps. They are available in a few local outlets, or you can get them mail-order for $12.

2 Exploring San Francisco

Orientation

*By Toni
Chapman*

Few cities in the world cram so much diversity into so little space. San Francisco is a relatively small city, with fewer than 750,000 residents nested on a 46.6-square-mile tip of land between San Francisco Bay and the Pacific Ocean.

San Franciscans cherish the city's colorful past, and many older buildings have been spared from demolition and nostalgically converted into modern offices and shops. For more than a century, the port city has been trafficking the peoples of the world. Today the city is again establishing strong commercial relations with the nations of the Pacific Rim. The unusually large number of residents with ties to other cultures flavors the cuisine, commerce, and charisma of the city. It also encourages a tolerance for deviations in customs and beliefs.

It's no accident that the San Francisco Bay Area has been a center for the environmental movement. An awareness of geographical setting permeates San Francisco life, with ever-present views of the surrounding mountains, ocean, and bay. Much of the city's neighborhood vitality comes from the distinct borders provided by its hills and valleys, and many areas are so named: Nob Hill, Russian Hill, Noe Valley. San Francisco neighborhoods are self-aware, and they retain strong cultural, political, and ethnic identities. Locals know this pluralism is the real life of the city. If you want to experience San Francisco, don't just stay downtown—visit the neighborhoods.

To do so you must navigate a maze of one-way streets and restricted parking zones. Public parking garages or lots tend to be expensive, as are the hotel parking spaces. The famed 40-plus hills can be a problem for drivers who are new to the terrain. People who know the city agree that one of the best ways to see and experience its many moods and neighborhoods is by foot. Those museums on wheels—the cable cars—or the numerous buses or trolleys can take you to or near many of the area's attractions. In the exploring tours that follow, we have often included information on public transportation.

Hills are a daily challenge to visitor and resident alike; good walking shoes are essential. Climate, too, is a consideration in deciding what to wear. There are dramatic temperature changes, especially in summer, when the afternoon fog rolls in. Winds are often a problem, both on the bay and cityside. Year-round, layered clothing best adapts to changing conditions; a cap or scarf and sunglasses are useful. Casual city togs are appropriate; shorts and tank tops are for southern California's climate.

Numbers in the margin correspond to points of interest on the Downtown San Francisco map.

Tour 1: Union Square

Since 1850 Union Square has been the heart of San Francisco's downtown. Its name derives from a series of violent pro-Union demonstrations staged in this hilly area just prior to the Civil War. This area is where you will find the city's finest department stores and its most elegant boutiques. There are 40 hotels within a three-block walk of the square, and the downtown theater district is nearby.

The square itself is a 2.6-acre oasis planted with palms, boxwood, and seasonal flowers, peopled with a kaleidoscope of characters: office workers sunning and brown-bagging, street musicians, always at least one mime, several vocal and determined preachers, and the ever-increasing parade of panhandlers. Smartly dressed women and camera-laden tourists usually hurry past the denizens. Throughout the year, the square hosts numerous public events: fashion shows, free noontime concerts, ethnic celebrations, and noisy demonstrations. Auto and bus traffic is often gridlocked on the four streets bordering the square. Post, Stockton, and Geary are one-way, while Powell runs in both directions until it crosses Geary, where it then becomes a one-way street to Market Street. Union Square covers a convenient but costly four-story underground garage. Close to 3,000 cars use it on busy holiday shopping and strolling days.

❶ Any visitor's first stop should be the **San Francisco Visitors Information Center** (tel. 415/391–2000) on the lower level of Hallidie Plaza at

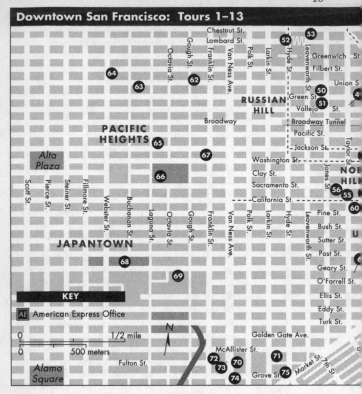

Downtown San Francisco: Tours 1–13

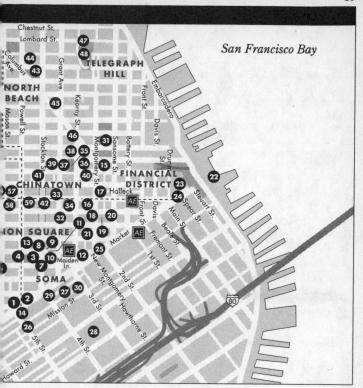

San Francisco Bay

Chestnut St.
Lombard St.
Columbus Ave.
Grant Ave.
TELEGRAPH HILL
NORTH BEACH
Mason St.
Powell St.
Kearny St.
Stockton St.
Front St.
Davis St.
Embarcadero
Battery St.
Sansome St.
Montgomery St.
Drumm St.
FINANCIAL DISTRICT
Halleck
Stewart St.
Spear St.
Main St.
Davis St.
Front St.
CHINATOWN
NION SQUARE
Market
Beale St.
Fremont St.
1 st St.
Maiden Ln.
SOMA
2nd St.
New Montgomery St.
3rd St.
Hawthorne St.
Mission St.
4th St.
5th St.
Howard St.
80

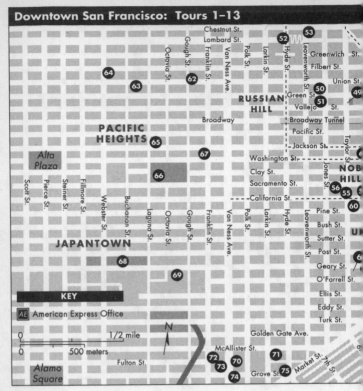

Downtown San Francisco: Tours 1–13

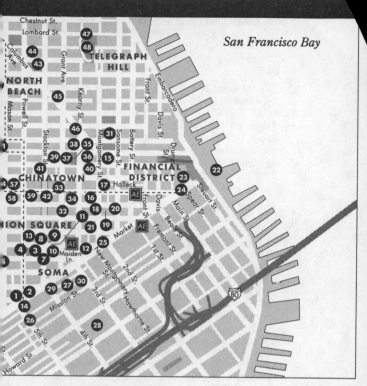

Powell and Market streets. It is open daily, and
the multilingual staff will answer specific questions as well as provide maps, brochures, and information on daily events. The office provides
24-hour recorded information (tel. 415/391–
2001).

② The **cable-car terminus,** also at Powell and Market streets, is the starting point for two of the
three operating lines. The Powell-Mason line
climbs up Nob Hill, then winds through North
Beach to Fisherman's Wharf. The Powell-Hyde
car also crosses Nob Hill, but then continues up
Russian Hill and down Hyde Street to Victorian
Park across from the Buena Vista Cafe and near
Ghirardelli Square.

Andrew Hallidie introduced the system in 1873
when he demonstrated his first car on Clay
Street. In 1964 the tramlike vehicles were designated national historic landmarks. Before 1900
there were 600 cable cars spanning a network of
100 miles. Today there are 39 cars in the three
lines, and the network covers just 12 miles. Most
of the cars date from the last century, although
the cars and lines had a complete $58 million
overhaul during the early 1980s. There are seats
for about 30 passengers, with usually that number standing or strap-hanging. If possible, plan
your cable car ride for mid-morning or mid-
afternoon during the week to avoid crowds. In
summertime there are often long lines to board
any of the three systems. (*See* Getting Around
by Cable Car in Chapter 1.)

③ A two-block stroll north along bustling Powell
Street leads to **Union Square** with its fashionable stores, fine hotels, and photogenic flower
stalls. At center stage, the Victory Monument
by Robert Ingersoll Aitken commemorates
Commodore George Dewey's victory over the
Spanish fleet at Manila in 1898. The 97-foot Co-
rinthian column, topped by a bronze figure sym-
bolizing naval conquest, was dedicated by
President Theodore Roosevelt in 1903 and with-
stood the 1906 earthquake.

After the earthquake and fire in 1906, the
square was dubbed "Little St. Francis" because
of the temporary shelter erected for residents of

the St. Francis Hotel. The actor John Barry-more was among the guests pressed into volun-teering to stack bricks in the square. His uncle, thespian John Drew, remarked, "It took an act of God to get John out of bed and the United States government to get him to work."

④ The **Westin St. Francis Hotel,** on the southwest corner of Post and Powell, was built here in 1904 and was gutted by the 1906 disaster. The sec-ond-oldest hotel in the city was conceived by Charles Crocker and his associates as an elegant hostelry for their millionaire friends. Swift service and sumptuous surroundings were hall-marks of the property. A sybarite's dream, the hotel's Turkish baths had ocean water piped in. A new, larger, more luxurious residence was opened in 1907 to attract loyal clients from among the world's rich and powerful. Today you can relax over a traditional teatime or opt for champagne and caviar in the dramatic Art Deco Compass Rose lounge in the lobby. Elaborate Chinese screens, secluded seating alcoves, and soothing background music make it an ideal time-out after frantic shopping or sightseeing. For dining, before or after the theater (within walking distance), visit the award-winning Vic-tor's. After a breathtaking ride up 30-plus stor-ies in an outside, glass-walled elevator, guests enter a warm, wood-paneled lobby area with re-cessed bookshelves housing leather-bound clas-sics. Floor-to-ceiling windows offer spectacular views of the bay and the city. Superb California cuisine is enhanced by a select list of California and French wines.

⑤ Both the Geary and Curran theaters are a few blocks west on Geary Street. The **Geary** (415 Geary St., tel. 415/749–2228) is home of the American Conservatory Theatre. Now in its 26th season, A.C.T. is one of North America's leading repertory companies. The 1,300-seat house normally offers a 34-week season to 20,000 subscribers, presenting both classical and contemporary dramas. The theater was closed indefinitely as a result of the October 1989 earthquake, and currently productions are being run at the Stage Door theater (420 Mason St.) and elsewhere until repairs are complete.
⑥ Its main box office remains open. The **Curran**

(445 Geary St., tel. 415/474–3800) is noted for showcasing traveling companies of Broadway shows.

7 The **San Francisco Ticket Box Office Service** (STBO, tel. 415/433–STBS) has a booth on the Stockton Street side of Union Square, opposite Maiden Lane. Open from noon till 7:30 PM, Tuesday through Saturday, it provides day-of-performance tickets (cash or traveler's checks only) to all types of performing arts events at half price, as well as regular full-price box-office services. Telephone reservations are not accepted.

Just a dash up from STBS, the newly renovated **8** **Grand Hyatt San Francisco** (345 Stockton St.) offers exciting city views from its lounge, the Club 36. Stop and examine sculptor Ruth Asawa's fantasy fountain honoring the city's hills, bridges, and unusual architecture plus a wonder world of real and mythical creatures. Children and friends helped the artist shape the hundreds of tiny figures created from baker's clay and then assembled on 41 large panels from which molds were made for the bronze casting. Asawa's distinctive designs decorate many public areas in the city. You can see her famous mermaid fountain at Ghirardelli Square.

9 Across the street is the small, deluxe **Campton Place Hotel** (340 Stockton St.). Opened in 1983, it is the ultimate in sumptuous furnishings, quiet elegance, and superior service. The dining room is a palette of peach, ivory, and gray tones; fresh flowers and handsome table appointments create a charming ambience.

10 Pop around the corner into **Maiden Lane,** which runs from Stockton to Kearny streets. Known as Morton Street in the raffish Barbary Coast era, this red-light district reported at least one murder a week. But the 1906 fire destroyed the brothels and the street emerged as Maiden Lane. It has since become a chic and costly mall. The two blocks are closed to vehicles from 11 AM until 4 PM. During the day, take-out snacks can be enjoyed while resting under the gay, umbrella-shaded tables. Masses of daffodils and bright blossoms and balloons bedeck the lane during the annual spring festival. A carnival mood prevails, with zany street musicians, artsy-craftsy people, and throngs of spectators.

⑪ Note **140 Maiden Lane:** This handsome brick structure is the only Frank Lloyd Wright building in San Francisco. With its circular interior ramp and skylights, it is said to have been a model for his designs for the Guggenheim Museum in New York. It now houses the Circle Gallery, a showcase of contemporary artists. Be sure to study the unique limited-edition art jewelry designed by internationally acclaimed Erté. *Open Mon.–Sat. 10–6, Sun. 11–5.*

⑫ The **Crocker Galleria** (Post and Kearny Sts., tel. 415/392–0100) is an imaginatively designed three-level complex of fine dining and shopping establishments capped by a dazzling glass dome. One block north of Kearny, Sutter Street is lined by prestigious art galleries, antiques dealers, smart hotels, and noted designer boutiques. Art Deco aficionados will want to linger at the striking medical/dental office building at ⑬ **450 Sutter Street.** Handsome Mayan-inspired designs are used in both exterior and interior surfaces of the 1930 terra-cotta-colored skyscraper.

Time Out Most stores and shops here open at about 9:30–10 AM. Venturing out early and settling down to a leisurely breakfast before the day's traffic and shoppers hit in full force is a nice way to ease into a busy day of sightseeing. **Mama's** (398 Geary St.) has always been a favorite for either light or full-breakfast selections. Or blow the day's meal budget at **Campton Place Hotel.** Wonderful breads and muffins, delicious hash, and out-of-season fruits are lavishly served. *340 Stockton St., tel. 415/781–5155. Reservations advised for brunch. Open weekdays 7–11 AM, Sat. 8–11:30 AM, Sun. brunch 8 AM–2:30 PM.*

Most of San Francisco's leading fine-art galleries are located around Union Square. Several are in the newly restored building at 49 Grant Avenue, where **Frankel** (tel. 415/981–2661, open Tues.–Fri. 10:30–5:30, Sat. 11–5) and **Robert Koch** (tel. 415/421–0122, open 11–5:30) showcase contemporary and historic photographs.

Serious shoppers will find the entire Union Square area richly rewarding. Bordering the square itself are leading department and specialty stores. **I. Magnin & Co.**, on the south side of Union Square at Stockton Street, is noted for its designer fashions, magnificent fur salon, and in-house fine jeweler, Laykin & Cie. Just across Stockton Street is the checkerboard-faced **Neiman Marcus**, opened in 1982. Philip Johnson's controversial design replaced an old San Francisco favorite, the City of Paris; all that remains is the great glass dome. **Macy's**, with entrances on Geary, Stockton, and O'Farrell streets, has huge selections of clothing for all members of the family, plus extensive furniture and household accessories departments. The men's department—one of the world's largest—occupies its own building across Stockton Street. Opposite is the new **FAO Schwarz** children's store, with its extravagant assortment of life-size stuffed animals, animated displays, and steep prices. **Saks Fifth Avenue**, at the northwest corner of the square at Post and Powell streets, still caters to the upscale shopper. Nearby are the pricey international boutiques of Hermes of Paris, Gucci, Celine of Paris, Alfred Dunhill, Louis Vuitton, and Cartier. (*See* Chapter 3.)

Across Market Street from the cable car turnaround, the rehabilitated corner of 5th Street is now occupied by the gleaming **San Francisco Centre**. Opened in October 1988, this urban mall is anchored by the huge **Nordstrom's** department store. Its glass-topped circular court and spiral escalators lead to more than 35 other stores. Foot-weary shoppers can rejuvenate themselves at **Spa Nordstrom** on the fifth floor, or lunch in the **City Centre Grille**, overlooking Market Street.

Tour 2: The Financial District

The heart of San Francisco's financial district is Montgomery Street. It was here in 1848 that Sam Brannan proclaimed the historic gold discovery on the American River. At that time, all the streets below Montgomery between California and Broadway were wharves. At least 100 ships were abandoned by frantic crews and passengers all caught up in the '49 gold fever. Many of the wrecks served as warehouses or were used as foundations for new constructions.

The financial district is roughly bordered by Kearny Street on the west, Washington Street on the north, and Market Street on the southeast. On workdays it is a congested canyon of soaring skyscrapers, gridlock traffic, and bustling pedestrians. In the evenings and on weekends the quiet streets allow walkers to admire the distinctive architecture. Unfortunately, the museums in corporate headquarters are closed then.

The city's most photographed high rise is the 853-foot **Transamerica Pyramid** at 600 Montgomery Street, between Clay and Washington streets at the end of Columbus Avenue. Designed by William Pereira and Associates in 1972, the $34 million controversial symbol has become more acceptable to local purists since it has gained San Francisco instant recognition worldwide. There is a public viewing area on the 27th floor (open weekdays 8–4). You can relax in a redwood grove along the east side of the building.

The granite and marble **Bank of America** building dominates the territory bounded by California, Pine, Montgomery, and Kearny streets. The 52-story polished red granite complex is crowned by a chic cocktail and dining restaurant. As in almost all corporate headquarters, the interiors display impressive original art, while outdoor plazas include avant-garde sculptures. A massive abstract black granite sculpture designed by the Japanese artist Masayuki in the mall has been dubbed the "Banker's Heart" by local wags.

Soaring 52 stories above the financial district, the Bank of America's **Carnelian Room** (tel. 415/ 433–7500) offers elegant and pricey dining with a nighttime view of the city lights. This is an excellent spot for a drink at sunset. By day, the room is the exclusive Banker's Club, open to members or by invitation. For a Chinese dinner with a French touch, try **Tommy Toy's** (655 Montgomery St.). Toy has re-created the opulent splendor of the 19th-century Empress Dowager's reading room. (The prices reflect the decor.)

(17) Diagonally across Montgomery Street is the **Wells Fargo Bank History Museum.** There were no formal banks in San Francisco during the early years of the Gold Rush, and miners often entrusted their gold dust to saloon keepers. In 1852 Wells Fargo opened its first bank in the city, and the company established banking offices in the Mother Lode camps using stagecoaches and pony express riders to service the burgeoning state. (California's population had boomed from 15,000 to 200,000 between 1848 and 1852.) The History Museum displays samples of nuggets and gold dust from major mines, a mural-size map of the Mother Lode, original art by Western artists Charlie Russell and Maynard Dixon, mementos of the poet bandit Black Bart, and letters of credit and old bank drafts. The showpiece is the red, century-old Concord stagecoach, which in the mid-1850s carried 15 passengers from St. Louis to San Francisco in three weeks. *420 Montgomery St. Admission free. Open banking days 9–5.*

(18) The **Russ Building** (235 Montgomery St.) was called "the skyscraper" when it was built in 1927. The Gothic design was modeled after the Chicago Tribune Tower, and until the 1960s was San Francisco's tallest—at just 31 stories. Prior to the 1906 earthquake and fire, the site was occupied by the Russ House, considered one of the finest hostelries in the city.

(19) The **Mills Building and Tower** (220 Montgomery St.) was the outstanding prefire building in the financial district. The 10-story all-steel construction had its own electric plant in the basement. The original Burnham and Root design of white marble and brick was erected in 1891–92. Damage from the 1906 fire was slight; its walls were somewhat scorched but were easily refurbished. Two compatible additions east on Bush Street were added in 1914 and 1918 by Willis Polk, and in 1931 a 22-story tower completed the design.

Ralph Stackpole's monumental 1930 granite sculptural groups, *Earth's Fruitfulness* and *Man's Inventive Genius*, flank another impos-

(20) ing structure, the **Pacific Stock Exchange** (which dates from 1915), on the south side of Pine Street at Sansome Street. The Stock Exchange Tower around the corner at 155 Sansome Street is a 1930 modern classic by architects Miller and Pfleuger, featuring an Art Deco gold ceiling and black marble-walled entry. *Pacific Stock Exchange, 301 Pine St., 94104, tel. 415/393–4000. Tours by 2-week advance reservation; minimum 8 persons.*

(21) Stroll down Sansome Street and turn right on Sutter Street. The **Hallidie Building** (130 Sutter St. between Kearny and Montgomery Sts.) was built as an investment by the University of California Regents in 1918 and named for cable car inventor and university regent Andrew S. Hallidie. It is believed to be the world's first all-glass-curtain-wall structure. Architect Willis Polk's revolutionary design hangs a foot beyond the reinforced concrete of the frame. It dominates the block with its reflecting glass, decorative exterior fire escapes that appear to be metal balconies, the Venetian Gothic cornice, and horizontal ornamental bands of birds at feeders.

Time Out At lunchtime on weekdays you can rub elbows with power brokers and politicians in venerable **Jack's Restaurant** (615 Sacramento St., tel. 415/986–9854). Opened in 1864 and a survivor of the quake, Jack's is a purveyor of traditional American fare—steaks, chops, seafood, and stews. Reservations are suggested. For excellent fresh seafood, San Franciscans in the know go to **Sam's Grill** (374 Bush St., tel. 415/421–0594). It's so popular for lunch you must arrive before 11:30 for even a chance at a table. Dinner service stops at 8:30, and Sam's is closed on weekends.

Tour 3: The Embarcadero and Lower Market Street

In one instance, the 1989 Loma Prieta earthquake changed San Francisco for the better: The Embarcadero freeway had to be torn down, making the foot of Market Street clearly visible for the first time in 30 years. The trademark of (22) the port is the quaint **Ferry Building** that stands at the Embarcadero. The clock tower is 230 feet high and was modeled by Arthur Page Brown after the campanile of Seville's cathedral. The four great clock faces on the tower, powered by the swinging action of a 14-foot pendulum, stopped at 5:17 on the morning of April 18, 1906, and stayed that way for the following 12 months. The 1896 building survived the quake and is now the headquarters of the Port Authority and the World Trade Center. A waterfront promenade that extends from this point to the Oakland Bay Bridge is great for jogging, watching the sailboats on the bay (if the day is not too windy), or enjoying a picnic. Check out the beautiful new pedestrian pier adjacent to Pier 1, with its old-fashioned lamps, wrought-iron benches, and awe-inspiring views of the bay. Ferries from behind the Ferry Building sail to Sausalito, Larkspur, and Tiburon.

㉓ Strolling back up Market Street, one's attention is drawn to the huge **Embarcadero Center** complex. Frequently called "Rockefeller Center West," its eight buildings include more than 100 shops, 40 restaurants, and two hotels, as well as high-rise residential towers and town-house condos. A three-tiered pedestrian mall links the buildings, and much attention has been given to attractive landscaping throughout the development. Louise Nevelson's dramatic 54-foot-high black-steel sculpture, "Sky Tree," stands guard over Building 3.

Time Out **Splendido's** (Embarcadero Center Four, tel. 415/986–3222) is a comfortable Mediterranean inn nestled amid the high rises. Its Italianate California cuisine, featuring fresh grilled meats and unusual marinades, has made this spot an instant classic. Lunch is the most popular meal here, and it is always very crowded, so try to reserve ahead.

㉔ The **Hyatt Regency Hotel** (5 Embarcadero) was designed by John Portman and is noted for its spectacular lobby and 20-story hanging garden. Just in front of the hotel is the **Justin Herman Plaza**. There are arts and crafts shows, street musicians, and mimes here on weekends year-round. Kite-flying is popular here. A huge concrete sculpture, the **Vaillancourt Fountain**, has had legions of critics since its installation in 1971; most of the time the fountain does not work, and many feel it is an eyesore.

25 The venerable **Sheraton-Palace Hotel** was recently restored and has resumed its place among San Francisco's grandest. Opened in 1875, the hotel was one of the city's most elegant lodging facilities. Destroyed by fire following the 1906 earthquake, it was rebuilt in 1909 and reopened on the site at Market and New Montgomery streets. More than $135 million has been spent on renovations, which included the restoration of the sumptuous glass-domed Garden Court and the installation of original mosaic tile floors in Oriental-rug designs. Maxfield Parrish's wall-size painting, *The Pied Piper*, graces the wall in the hotel's Pied Piper Room.

26 The **Old San Francisco Mint,** at 5th and Mission streets, reopened as a museum in 1973. The century-old brick-and-stone building exhibits a priceless collection of gold coins. Visitors tour the vaults and can strike their own souvenir medal on an 1869 press. *Admission free. Open weekdays 10–4.*

Tour 4: South of Market (SoMa)

The vast tract of downtown land south of Market Street along the waterfront and west to the Mission district is now known by the acronym SoMa (patterned after New York City's south-of-Houston SoHo). Formerly known as South of the Slot because of the cable-car slot that ran up Market Street, the area has a history of housing recent immigrants to the city—beginning with tents set up in 1848 by the gold-rush miners and continuing for decades. Except for a brief flowering of English-inspired elegance during the mid-19th century in the pockets of South Park and Rincon Hill, the area was reserved for newcomers who couldn't yet afford to move to another neighborhood. Industry took over most of the area when the big earthquake collapsed most of the homes into their quicksand bases.

Ten years ago the San Francisco Redevelopment Agency grabbed 87 acres of run-down downtown land, leveled anything that stood on them, and began the largest building program in the

27 city's history: **Yerba Buena Center.** More than
$1.5 billion will be used to bring new develop-
ments onto the site. Much of the project is still in
the blue-print stage, but it will eventually include, along with the already completed Marriott Hotel and the recently expanded Moscone
Convention Center, the new Museum of Modern
Art, a performing arts theater, and a rarity for
downtown—open space. The neighborhood has
already been transformed in unforeseen ways.
As soon as the Moscone Convention Center was
completed in 1981, the area became a focal point
for cultural and architectural urban gentrifica-
tion.

For years industrial South of Market had been a
stomping ground for the gay leather set, and a
dozen bars frequented by the group had existed
alongside warehouses and small factories. But
the increasing visibility of gay culture, joined
with redevelopment fervor, gave South of Market a social sanction it hadn't had for a hundred
years. In the wake of the AIDS crisis, most of
the area's gay bars have given way to trendy
straight bars. Within a few years, South of Market has been transformed into SoMa, a center
for San Francisco nightclubbing, dining, and
gallery hopping.

There are really two SoMas, one during the day
and the other at night; one for businesspeople,
the other for the (mostly young) leisure class.
28 The **Moscone Convention Center,** on Howard
Street between 3rd and 4th streets, remains the
centerpiece of the redevelopment area. It is distinguished by a contemporary glass-and-girder
lobby at street level (most of the exhibit space is
underground) and a monolithic, column-free interior that was the site of the 1984 Democratic
convention. In 1992 the center finished a $150
million expansion project that doubled its size
and incorporated a new building across Howard
Street with underground exhibit space. Construction of the remainder of Yerba Buena Center, around Moscone Center, is expected to
continue through 1994.

Up 4th Street from the Moscone Convention
29 Center you can't miss the new **San Francisco
Marriott at Moscone Center** (777 Market St.),

the architectural curiosity that had the city in an uproar when it opened in 1989. Its 40-story ziggurat construction topped with reflecting glass pinwheels elicited gasps from newspaper columnists and passersby alike, earning it comparisons with a juke box, a high-rise parking meter, and a giant rectal thermometer. It takes its civic place in a long line of blooper buildings in The City (the Transamerica pyramid; the old Jack Tar—now the Cathedral Hill—Hotel; and the San Francisco Federal Building) that keep the city talking and passing newer and newer building ordinances. Whether San Franciscans will come to embrace the building—as they have the Transamerica pyramid—is an open question; what's certain is that the hotel's 1,500 rooms already lure many of the city's 500,000 yearly visiting conventioneers. The new Marriott contains the city's largest ballroom, a complete health spa, and seven restaurants.

30 One block away, the deluxe 32-story **ANA Hotel** (50 3rd St.), formerly the Meridien San Francisco, was itself a building of some architectural controversy, placed crosswise at the end of its street. Japanese-owned ANA Hotels purchased the hotel in 1991 and undertook a $28 million renovation in 1992.

For daytime activities the rest of SoMa may be considered "under construction," but for nighttime entertainment it's ready to go. The hottest area is around 11th Street, with its mix of nightclubs and restaurants. **Club O,** formerly The Oasis (11th and Folsom Sts., tel. 415/621–8119), was the club that started luring straights back to a predominantly gay neighborhood, with its pool-on-the-premises parties and live music. The **DNA Lounge** (375 11th St., tel. 415/626–1409) has a more aggressive new-wave attitude, and at the **Paradise Lounge** (11th and Folsom Sts., tel. 415/861–6906) you can catch such oddball specialty acts as chanteuse Connie Champagne and her Tiny Bubbles.

Slim's (333 11th St., tel. 415/621–3330) is Boz Scaggs' club, and with its focus on "American roots" rock/rhythm-and-blues music it should be around for a while.

Time Out There are several fine restaurants in the area, but for atmosphere none of them can compare with good ol' rockin' and rollin' **Hamburger Mary's**. The decor is funky, the music loud, the clientele polymorphous, and the thick hamburgers served on slices of nine-grain bread and piled high with grilled onions. Probably no place in the city has been able to mix straights and gays in the same place so successfully and keep the feeling of urban adventurousness bordering on party. *1582 Folsom St., tel. 415/626–5767. Open weekdays 11 AM–2 AM, weekends 10 AM–2 AM.*

SoMa is where artists live, hang out, and also show their work in several galleries on the cutting edge of San Francisco's art scene. **Artspace** (1286 Folsom St., tel. 415/626–9100) operates more like a museum than a gallery, highlighting new artists in a not-for-sale setting. **New Langton Arts** (1246 Folsom St., tel. 415/626–5416) is one of the city's longest-surviving alternative exhibit and performance spaces. Its focus is mixed-media and performance art, and it offers a provocative series of readings and talks. **Eye Gallery** (1151 Mission St., tel. 415/431–6911) and **San Francisco Camerawork** (70 12th St., tel. 415/621–1001), as their names imply, turn the light on up-and-coming photographers.

The **Ansel Adams Center** (250 4th St., tel. 415/495–7000) showcases both historical and contemporary photography, with a permanent collection of Adams's own work. *Admission: $4 adults, $3 students, $2 youths 12–17 and senior citizens, children under 12 free. Open Tues.–Sun. 11–6.*

A restaurant row has taken shape down Folsom Street between 7th and 8th streets. **Julie's Supper Club** (1123 Folsom St., tel. 415/861–0707) is the most distinctive, with its pink-and-black '50s decor, curved leatherette bar, and ambience designed for drinking martinis. **Eddie Jacks** (1151 Folsom St., tel. 415/626–2388) is internationally nouvelle; **Milano Joe's** (1175 Folsom St., tel. 415/861–2815) is a high-tech palace with northern Italian cooking; and the **Half Shell** (64 Rausch St., tel. 415/552–7677), in little Rausch alley, specializes in seafood. Be sure to

take a closer look at **Brain Wash** (1122 Folsom
St., tel. 415/431–9274), the very unique combi-
nation laundromat and café! Where else can you
go to socialize and get your housework done at
the same time?

In keeping with SoMa's tradition of being the
underside of the city, it now offers you the underside of shopping: **discount outlets.** On Saturdays, the small alleys between 3rd and 7th
streets and between Townsend and Harrison
streets are crowded with hungry shoppers looking to save that magic 50%. Start at 3rd Street
between Brannan and Townsend streets; there
are 20 discount shops at the 660 Center Arcade,
offering everything from designer fashions to
Icelandic sweaters. A few blocks south, near
China Basin, the casual emporium **Esprit** has its
huge outlet store, with a café for weary bargain-
hunters on the premises. *499 Illinois St., tel.
415/957–2550. Open weekdays 10–8, Sat. 10–7,
Sun. 11–5.*

Tour 5: Jackson Square

In the Gay Nineties San Francisco had earned
the title of "the Wickedest City in the World."
The saloons, dance halls, cheap hotels, and
brothels of its Barbary Coast attracted sailors
and gold rushers. Most of this red-light district
was destroyed in the 1906 fire; what remains is
31 now part of **Jackson Square.** A stroll through
this district recalls some of the romance and
rowdiness of early San Francisco.

Some of the city's earliest business buildings
still stand in the blocks of Jackson Square between Montgomery and Sansome streets. By
the end of World War II, most of the 1850 brick
structures had fallen on hard times. In 1951,
however, things changed. A group of talented,
preservation-minded designers and furniture
wholesale dealers selected the centrally located, depressed area for their showrooms. By
the 1970s, the reclaimed two- and three-story
renovated brick buildings were acclaimed nationwide. In 1972 the city officially designated
the area—bordered by Columbus Avenue on
the west, a line between Broadway and Pacific
Avenue on the north, Washington on the south,

and Sansome Street on the east—as San Francisco's first historic district. Seventeen buildings were given landmark status.

Jackson Square became the interior design center of the West. Unfortunately, property values soared, forcing many of the fabric and furniture outlets to move to the developing Potrero Hill section. Advertising agencies, attorneys, and antiques dealers now occupy the charming renovations.

The **Ghirardelli Chocolate Factory** was once housed at 415 Jackson. In 1857 Domenico Ghirardelli moved both his growing business and his family into this property. It was quite common for the upper floors of these buildings to be used as flats by either the building's owners or its tenants. By 1894 Ghirardelli had moved his expanding chocolate enterprise to Ghirardelli Square.

Another historic building is the former **A. P. Hotaling and Company whiskey distillery** at 451 Jackson. This handsome brick building retains the iron shutters installed in 1866 to "fireproof" the house.

Around the corner, south toward Washington, is the much-photographed compound at 722–28 **Montgomery Street**, headquarters of Melvin Belli, the "King of Torts," one of the nation's most flamboyant attorneys. Belli has rejuvenated these nostalgic relics with red plush and gaslight Victorian splendor. Neighbors have emulated this rich period decor.

The **Golden Era Building** at 732 Montgomery Street also dates from the 1850s. It was the home of the most substantial literary periodical published locally during the 1850s and 1860s. Mark Twain and Bret Harte were two of its celebrated contributors.

Time Out   Big windows, white walls, and chains of red peppers, garlic, and sausage set the stage for homemade pastas, charcoal-broiled seafood, and select wines, all of which make **Ciao** a special stop for lunch or dinner. *230 Jackson St., tel. 415/982–9500. Dinner reservations advised. AE, DC, MC, V. Open Mon.–Thurs. 11:30AM–*

11PM, Fri.–Sat. 11:30AM–midnight, Sun. 4PM–10:30.

The mood at **Ernie's** on Montgomery Street near Pacific Avenue is dramatically different. Its sumptuous Barbary Coast elegance, talented young chef, and outstanding wine selection have attracted the rich and famous for more than 25 years. *847 Montgomery St., tel. 415/397–5969. Reservations required. Dress: formal. AE, DC, MC, V. Open 11:30AM–2:30, 6:30–10.*

Tour 6: Chinatown

A city within a city, this is the largest Chinese community outside of Asia. Approximately 100,000 Chinese live in a 24-block downtown area just south of North Beach (and in the Richmond district's "New Chinatown"). Chinatown has been revitalized by the fairly recent immigration of Southeast Asians, who have added new character and life to the neighborhood. Downtown Chinatown is officially defined as an area reaching from Bay Street south to California Street and from Sansome Street at the edge of downtown west to Van Ness Avenue; these boundaries actually include much of Russian Hill and Nob Hill.

32 Visitors usually enter Chinatown through the green-tiled dragon-crowned **Chinatown Gate** at Bush Street and Grant Avenue. To best savor this district, explore it on foot (it's not far from Union Square), even though you may find the bustling, noisy, colorful stretches of Grant and Stockton streets north of Bush difficult to navigate. Parking is extremely hard to find, and traffic is impossible. As in Hong Kong, most families shop daily for fresh meats, vegetables, and bakery products. This street world shines with much good-luck crimson and gold; giant beribboned floral wreaths mark the opening of new bakeries, bazaars, and banks.

San Francisco has pioneered the resurrection of Chinese regional cooking for American palates. Cantonese cuisine, with its familiar staples of chow mein and chop suey (said to be invented in San Francisco by Gold Rush-era Chinese cooks) now exists alongside spicier Szechuan, Hunan, and Mandarin specialties. With almost 100 restaurants squeezed into a 14-block area, Chinatown offers plenty of food. In the windows of markets on Stockton Street and Grant Avenue you can see roast ducks hanging, fresh fish and shellfish swimming in tanks, and strips of Chinese-style barbecued pork shining in pink glaze. The streets are crowded day and night.

33 The handsome brick **Old St. Mary's Church** at Grant and California streets served as the city's Catholic cathedral until 1891. Granite quarried in China was used in the structure, which was dedicated in 1854. Diagonally across the inter-

34 section is **St. Mary's Park**, a tranquil setting for local sculptor Beniamino (Benny) Bufano's heroic stainless-steel and rose-colored granite Sun Yat Sen. The 12-foot statue of the founder of the Republic of China was installed in 1937. Bufano was born in Rome on October 14, 1898, and died in San Francisco on August 16, 1970. His stainless-steel and mosaic statue of St. Francis welcomes guests at San Francisco International Airport.

Shopping surrounds the stroller on **Grant Avenue**. Much of what is offered in the countless curio shops is worthless, and discerning visitors may be dismayed by the gaudy and glittery gimcrackery. In recent years, however, a growing number of large department-store-type operations have opened. Most feature an ever-growing array of products from the People's Republic. You'll find, too, that visiting the Chinese markets, even just window-gazing, is fascinating. Note the dragon-entwined lampposts, the pagoda roofs, and street signs with Chinese calligraphy.

The city's first house was built in 1836 at the corner of Grant Avenue and Clay Street; it was later destroyed in the 1906 earthquake. Turn right here and a short walk will take you to

35 **Portsmouth Square**, the potato patch that became the plaza for Yerba Buena. This is where Montgomery raised the American flag in 1846. Note the bronze galleon atop a nine-foot granite shaft. Designed by Bruce Porter, the sculpture was erected in 1919 in memory of Robert Louis Stevenson, who often visited the site during his

1879–80 residence. In the morning, the park is crowded with people performing solemn t'ai chi rituals.

36 From here you can walk to the **Chinese Cultural Center,** which frequently displays exhibits of Chinese-American artists as well as traveling exhibits of Chinese culture. The center also offers $12 Saturday-afternoon walking tours of historic points in Chinatown. *In the Holiday Inn, 750 Kearny St., tel. 415/986–1822. Admission free. Open Tues.–Sat. 10–4.*

You're now on the edge of North Beach and could easily walk over to the City Lights bookstore or other North Beach sites.

The original Chinatown burned down after the 1906 earthquake; the first building to set the style for the new Chinatown is near Portsmouth Square, at 743 Washington Street. The three-**37** tiered pagoda called the **Old Chinese Telephone Exchange** was built in 1909. Also worth a visit is **38** **Buddha's Universal Church,** 720 Washington Street, a five-story, hand-built temple decorated with murals and tile mosaics. *Open 2nd and 4th Sun. of the month, 1–3.*

Time Out Skip that Big Mac you've been craving; opt instead for dim sum, a variety of pastries filled with meat, fish, and vegetables, the Chinese version of a smorgasbord. More than a dozen Chinese restaurants feature this unusual lunch/brunch adventure from about 11 AM to 3 PM. In most places, stacked food-service carts patrol the premises; customers select from the varied offerings, and the final bill is tabulated by the number of different saucers on the table. Dim sum restaurants tend to be big, crowded, noisy, cheap, and friendly. Suggestions are often offered by nearby strangers as to what is inside the tempting morsels. Two favorites on Pacific Avenue, two blocks north of Washington Street, between Stockton and Powell streets, are **Hong Kong Tea House** (835 Pacific Ave.) and **Tung Fong** (808 Pacific Ave.). Many of the smaller, inexpensive Chinese restaurants and cafés do not accept credit cards; some serve beer and wine.

㊴ Waverly Place is noted for ornate painted balconies and Chinese temples. **Tien Hou Temple,** at 125 Waverly Place, was dedicated to the Queen of the Heavens and Goddess of the Seven Seas by Day Ju, one of the first three Chinese to arrive in San Francisco in 1852.

㊵ The **Chinese Historical Society** traces the history of Chinese immigrants and their contributions to the state's rail, mining, and fishing industries. *650 Commercial St. (near Sacramento and Montgomery Sts.), tel. 415/391–1188. Admission free. Open Wed.–Sun. 12–4.*

The other main thoroughfare in Chinatown, where locals shop for everyday needs, is Stockton Street, which parallels Grant Avenue. This is the real heart of Chinatown. Housewives jostle one another as they pick apart the sidewalk displays of Chinese vegetables. Double-parked trucks unloading crates of chickens or ducks add to the all-day traffic jams. You'll see excellent examples of Chinese architecture along this street. Most noteworthy is the elaborate **㊶ Chinese Six Companies** (843 Stockton St.) with its curved roof tiles and elaborate cornices. Folk-art murals grace the walls of an apartment building at Stockton Street and Pacific Avenue. Displays of jade and gold glitter from jewelry windows—the Chinese value these items above all other ornaments. It's an easy ½-hour walk back downtown to Union Square via the **㊷ Stockton Street Tunnel,** which runs from Sacramento Street to Sutter Street. Completed in 1914, this was the city's first tunnel to accommodate vehicular and pedestrian traffic.

Tour 7: North Beach and Telegraph Hill

Like neighboring Chinatown, North Beach, centered on Columbus Avenue north of Broadway, is best explored on foot. In the early days there truly was a beach. At the time of the Gold Rush, the bay extended into the hollow between Telegraph and Russian hills. North Beach, less than a square mile, is the most densely populated district in the city and is truly cosmopolitan. Much of the old-world ambience still lingers in this easygoing and polyglot neighborhood. Novelist Herbert Gold, a North Beach resident, calls the area "the longest running, most glorious American bohemian operetta outside Greenwich Village."

Like Chinatown, this is a section of the city where you can eat and eat. Restaurants, cafés, delis, and bakeries abound. Many Italian restaurants specialize in family-style full-course meals at reasonable prices. A local North Beach delicacy is focaccia—spongy pizzalike bread slathered with olive oil and chives or tomato sauce—sold fresh from the oven at quaint old **Liguria Bakery** at the corner of Stockton and Filbert streets. Eaten warm or cold, it is the perfect walking food.

Among the first immigrants to Yerba Buena during the early 1840s were young men from the northern provinces of Italy. By 1848, the village, renamed San Francisco, had become an overnight boomtown with the discovery of gold. Thousands more poured into the burgeoning area, seeking the golden dream. For many the trail ended in San Francisco. The Genoese started the still-active fishing industry, as well as much-needed produce businesses. Later the Sicilians emerged as leaders of the fishing fleets and eventually as proprietors of the seafood restaurants lining Fisherman's Wharf. Meanwhile, their Genoese cousins established banking and manufacturing empires.

43 **Washington Square** may well be the daytime social heart of what was once considered "Little Italy." By mid-morning, groups of conservatively dressed elderly Italian men are sunning and sighing at the state of their immediate world. Nearby, laughing Asian and Caucasian playmates race through the grass with Frisbees or colorful kites. Multinational denim-clad mothers exchange shopping tips and ethnic recipes. Elderly Chinese matrons stare impassively at the passing parade. Camera-toting tourists focus their lenses on the adjacent Romanesque

44 splendor of **Saints Peter and Paul,** often called the Italian Cathedral. Built in 1924, its twin-turreted terra-cotta towers are local landmarks. On the first Sunday of October, the annual Blessing of the Fleet is celebrated with a mass followed by a parade to Fisherman's

Wharf. Another popular annual event is the Columbus Day pageant.

The 1906 earthquake and fire devastated this area, and the park provided shelter for hundreds of the homeless. **Fior d'Italia**, facing the cathedral, is San Francisco's oldest Italian restaurant. The original opened in 1886 and continued to operate in a tent after the 1906 earthquake until new quarters were ready. Surrounding streets are packed with savory Italian delicatessens, bakeries, Chinese markets, coffeehouses, and ethnic restaurants. Wonderful aromas fill the air. (Coffee beans roasted at **Graffeo** at 733 Columbus Avenue are shipped to customers all over the United States.) Stop by the **Panelli Brothers deli** (1419 Stockton St.) for a memorable, reasonably priced meat-and-cheese sandwich to go. **Florence Ravioli Factory** (1412 Stockton St.) features garlic sausages, prosciutto, and mortadella, as well as 75 tasty cheeses and sandwiches to go. **Victoria** (1362 Stockton St.) has heavenly cream puffs and eclairs. Around the corner on Columbus Avenue is **Molinari's**, noted for the best salami in town and a mouthwatering array of salads. (There is usually a wait for service.)

South of Washington Square and just off Columbus Avenue is the **Church of Saint Francis of Assisi** (610 Vallejo St.). This 1860 Victorian Gothic building stands on the site of the frame parish church that served the Gold Rush Catholic community.

Over the years, North Beach has attracted creative individualists. The Beat Renaissance of the 1950s was born, grew up, flourished, then faltered in this then-predominantly Italian enclave. The Beat gathering places are gone, and few of the original leaders remain. Poet Lawrence Ferlinghetti still holds court at his **City Lights Bookstore** (261 Columbus Ave.). The face of North Beach is changing. The bohemian community has migrated up Grant Avenue above Columbus Avenue. Originally called Calle de la Fundacion, Grant Avenue is the oldest street in the city. Each June a street fair is held on the upper part of the avenue, where a cluster of cafés, boutiques, and galleries attract crowds.

Time Out   The richness of North Beach lifestyle is reflected in the neighborhood's numerous cafés. Breakfast at **Caffe Roma** (414 Columbus Ave.) and create your own omelet from a list of 11 ingredients. Skip the main room with its pastel murals of cherubs and settle at one of the umbrella-shaded tables on the patio. Moviemaker Francis Ford Coppola is a regular, and the adjoining **Millefiori Inn**, a charming bed-and-breakfast, frequently hosts film celebrities. Across the street is **Caffe Puccini** (411 Columbus Ave.). It could be Italy: Few of the staff speak English. Their *caffe latte* (coffee, chocolate, cinnamon, and steamed milk) and strains of Italian operas recall *Roman Holiday*. A Saturday morning must is around the corner at **Caffe Trieste** (601 Vallejo St.). Get there at about 11; at noon, the Giotta family's weekly musical begins. The program ranges from Italian pop and folk music to favorite family operas. The Trieste opened in 1956 and became headquarters for the area's beatnik poets, artists, and writers. **Caffe Malvina** (1600 Stockton St.), ideal for people-watching along Washington Square, started during the 1950s and was among the first U.S. importers of Italian-made espresso machines.

❹⓻   **Telegraph Hill** rises from the east end of Lombard Street to about 300 feet and is capped with the landmark Coit Tower, dedicated as a monument to the city's volunteer firefighters. Early during the Gold Rush, an eight-year-old who would become one of the city's most memorable eccentrics, Lillie Hitchcock Coit, arrived on the scene. Legend relates that at age 17, "Miss Lil" deserted a wedding party and chased down the street after her favorite engine, Knickerbocker No. 5, clad in her bridesmaid finery. She was soon made an honorary member of the Knickerbocker Company, and after that always signed herself "Lillie Coit 5" in honor of her favorite fire engine. Lillie died in 1929 at the age of 86, leaving the city about $100,000 of her million-dollar-plus estate to "expend in an appropriate manner . . . to the beauty of San Francisco."

Telegraph Hill residents command some of the best views in the city, as well as the most difficult ascent to their aeries. The Greenwich stairs

lead up to Coit Tower from Filbert Street, and
there are steps down to Filbert Street on the opposite side of Telegraph Hill. Views are superb
en route, but most visitors should either taxi up
to the tower or take the Muni bus No. 39 Coit at
Washington Square. To catch the bus from Union Square, walk to Stockton and Sutter streets,
board the Muni No. 30, and ask for a transfer to
use at Washington Square (Columbus Ave. and
Union St.) to board the No. 39 Coit. Public parking is very limited at the tower, and on holidays
and weekends there are long lines of cars and
buses winding up the narrow road.

48 **Coit Tower** stands as a monument not only to
Lillie Coit and the city's firefighters but also to
the influence of the political radical Mexican muralist Diego Rivera. Fresco was Rivera's medi-
um, and it was his style that unified the work of
most of the 25 artists who painted the murals in
the tower. The murals were commissioned by
the U.S. government as a Public Works of Art
Project. The artists were paid $38 a week. Some
were fresh from art schools; others found no
market for art in the dark depression days of the
early 1930s. An illustrated brochure for sale in
the tiny gift shop explains the various murals
dedicated to the workers of California. There is
an elevator to the top that provides a panoramic
view of both the Bay Bridge and Golden Gate
Bridge; directly offshore is the famous Alcatraz
and just behind it, Angel Island, a hikers' and
campers' paradise. Be sure to carry a camera
and binoculars. There are often artists at work
in Pioneer Park, at the foot of the tower. Small
paintings of the scene are frequently offered for
sale at modest prices. The impressive bronze
statue of Christopher Columbus, *Discoverer of
America*, was a gift of the local Italian community.

Walk down the Greenwich Steps east to Montgomery Street, and turn right. At the corner
where the Filbert Steps intersect, you'll find
the Art Deco masterpiece at 1360 Montgomery
Street. (*See* Off the Beaten Track, *below*.) Its
elegant etched-glass gazelle and palms coun-
terpoint the silvered fresco of the heroic
bridgeworker—echoed by an actual view of the
Bay Bridge in the distance. Descend the Filbert

Steps, amid roses, fuchsias, irises, and trumpet flowers, courtesy of Grace Marchant, who labored for nearly 30 years to transform a dump into one of San Francisco's hidden treasures. At the last landing before the final descent to Sansome Street, pause and sit on the bench to breathe in the fragrance of roses as you gaze at the bridge and bay below. A small bronze plaque set into the bench reads: "I have a feeling we're not in Kansas anymore."

At the foot of the hill you will come to the Levi Strauss headquarters, a carefully landscaped $150 million complex that appears so collegial and serene it is affectionately known as LSU (Levi Strauss University). Fountains and grassy knolls complement the stepped-back redbrick buildings and provide a stress-reducing environment perfect for brown-bag lunches.

Time Out You can choose the ingredients for an urban picnic at **Il Fornaio** (in the Plaza, 1265 Battery St., tel. 415/986–0100). The **Uno Poco di Tutti** deli offers a variety of cold pasta salads and such treats as giant artichokes stuffed with bread crumbs and capers. A bakery will provide you with Italian sweets, or you can eat in the dining room, choosing from the house specialties: meats from the rotisserie or pizzas from the oak-fired ovens. Down Battery Street, the **Fog City Diner** has attracted the city's young professionals since it opened in 1985. The menu is basically down-home American; native diners recommend the crab cakes. Make reservations, even for a late lunch. The prices are moderate and the atmosphere is comfortable. *1300 Battery St., tel. 415/982–2000. Open Sun.–Thurs. 11:30 AM–11 PM, Fri.–Sat. 11:30 AM–midnight.*

Tour 8: Russian Hill

Just nine blocks or so from downtown, Russian Hill has long been home to old San Francisco families and, during the 1890s, to a group of bohemian artists and writers that included Charles Norris, George Sterling, and Maynard Dixon. An old legend says that during San Francisco's early days the steep hill (294 feet high) was the site of a cemetery for Russian seal hunters and traders. Now the hills are covered with an astounding array of housing: simple studios, sumptuous pied-à-terres, Victorian flats, and costly boxlike condos.

At Union Square, board the Powell-Mason cable car and hop off at Vallejo and Mason streets. This will put you at an ideal spot from which to photograph Alcatraz Island and the bay. Slowly start climbing the Vallejo Steps up to attractive **49 Ina Coolbrith Park.** An Oakland librarian and poet, Ina introduced both Jack London and Isadora Duncan to the world of books. For years she entertained literary greats in her Macondray Lane home (near the park). In 1915 she was named poet laureate of California.

A number of buildings in this neighborhood survived the 1906 earthquake and fire and still stand today. The house at **1652 Taylor Street** was saved by alert fire fighters who spotted the American flag on the property and managed to quench the flames using seltzer water and wet sand. A number of brown-shingle structures on Vallejo Street designed by Willis Polk, one of the city's most famous architects, also survived. For years, the Polk family resided at **1013 Vallejo Street.** Stroll past **1034–1036 Vallejo**—both buildings, tucked in between new million-dollar condominium neighbors, were designed by Polk.

At this point, two secluded alleys beckon: To the north, **Russian Hill Place** has a row of Mediterranean-style town houses designed by Polk in 1915. On **Florence Place** to the south, 1920s stucco survivors reign over more contemporary construction.

Follow Vallejo Street west to Jones Street, turn right, and continue on to Green Street. The 1000 block of Green, on one of the three crests of Russian Hill, is one of the most remarkable blocks in **50** San Francisco. The **Feusier House** (1067 Green St.), built in 1857 and now a private residence, is one of two octagonal houses left in the city. On the other side of the street (at 1088) is the **1907 firehouse.** Local art patron Mrs. Ralph K. Davies bought it from the city in 1956. There is a small museum, and the property is often used for charity benefits.

Continue west on Green Street to Hyde Street, where the Hyde-Powell cable car line runs. Turn right and stroll up to Union Street. (If you're tired of walking, stop at the original Swensen's for an ice-cream treat.) At this point you have two options: You can meander down Union Street to Jones Street, turn right and walk a few steps down to magical **Macondray Lane**, a quiet cobbled pedestrian street lined with Edwardian cottages. From a flight of steep wooden stairs that lead down to Taylor Street you'll get some spectacular views of the bay. From Taylor Street it is then a short walk downhill to North Beach.

Your other option is to keep walking north on Hyde Street three blocks to **Lombard Street.** Stretching the length of just one block, San Francisco's "crookedest street" drops down the east face of Russian Hill in eight switchbacks to Leavenworth Street. Few tourists with cars can resist the lure of the scary descent. Pedestrians should be alert while using the steep steps, especially when photographing the smashing views.

At the base of the steps, turn left on Leavenworth Street and then right on Chestnut Street. At 800 Chestnut Street is the **San Francisco Art Institute.** Established in 1871, it occupied the Mark Hopkins home at California and Mason streets from 1893 to 1906. The school carried on in temporary quarters until 1926, when the present Spanish Colonial building was erected on the top of Russian Hill. Be sure to see the impressive seven-sectioned fresco painted in 1931 by the Mexican master Diego Rivera. There are also frequent exhibitions of student efforts.

From here you can walk back to Hyde Street and take the cable car back downtown or walk a few blocks north to the wharf. Hardy walkers will probably prefer to walk down to Columbus Avenue and then west on North Point or Beach streets to Ghirardelli Square, the Cannery, and Aquatic Park.

Tour 9: Nob Hill

If you don't mind climbing uphill, Nob Hill is within walking distance of Union Square. Once called the Hill of Golden Promise, it became Nob Hill during the 1870s when "the Big Four"—Charles Crocker, Leland Stanford, Mark Hopkins, and Collis Huntington—built their hilltop estates. It is still home to many of the city's elite as well as four of San Francisco's finest hotels.

In 1882 Robert Louis Stevenson called Nob Hill "the hill of palaces." But the 1906 earthquake and fire destroyed all the palatial mansions. The shell of one survived. The Flood brownstone (1000 California St.) was built by the Comstock silver baron in 1886 at a reputed cost of $1.5 million. In 1909 the property was purchased by the **⑤④** prestigious **Pacific Union Club.** The 45-room exclusive club remains the bastion of the wealthy and powerful. Adjacent is a charming small park noted for its frequent art shows.

⑤⑤ Neighboring **Grace Cathedral** (1051 Taylor St.) is the seat of the Episcopal Church in San Francisco. The soaring Gothic structure took 53 years to build. The gilded bronze doors at the east entrance were taken from casts of Ghiberti's Gates of Paradise on the baptistery in Florence. The superb rose window is illuminated at night. There are often organ recitals on Sundays at 5 PM, as well as special programs during the holiday seasons.

⑤⑥ The huge **Masonic Auditorium** (1111 California St.) is also the site of frequent musical events, including "Today's Artists," a concert series that highlights young classical musicians.

⑤⑦ What sets the **Fairmont Hotel** (California and Mason Sts.) apart from other luxury hotels is its legendary history. Since its dazzling opening in 1907, the opulent marble palace has hosted presidents, royalty, and local nabobs. The lobby sports as much plush red-velvet upholstery as anyone could ever want to see. The eight-room $6,000-a-night penthouse suite was used frequently in the TV series *Hotel*, and the stunning Nob Hill Spa and Fitness Club is on the premises.

⑤⑧ The stately **Mark Hopkins Inter-Continental Hotel,** across California Street, is remembered fondly by thousands of World War II veterans who jammed the Top of the Mark lounge before

leaving for overseas duty. At California and
59 Powell streets stands the posh **Stouffer Stanford
Court Hotel,** a world-class establishment known
for service and personal attention. The structure is a remodeled 1909 apartment house.

60 The **Huntington** (1075 California St.) is impecca-
bly British in protecting the privacy of its celebrated guests.

61 The **Cable Car Museum** (Washington and Mason
Sts.) exhibits photographs, scale models, and
other memorabilia from the cable car system's
115-year history. A new 17-minute film is shown
continually. *Tel. 415/474–1887. Admission free.
Open daily 10–5.*

Tour 10: Union Street

Union Street, west of Van Ness Avenue, was the
first shopping street in San Francisco to reno-
vate its gingerbread Victorians into trendy boutiques, galleries, and restaurants. Known
colloquially as Cow Hollow because it was once a
rural settlement with small farms, pastures,
and resident dairy herds, the area is now known
for great shopping, dining, and drinking.

To get to Union Street, take either Muni bus No.
45 from Sutter Street or bus No. 41 from North
Beach's Washington Square. Get off at Gough
Street and begin walking west. Note the his-
62 toric **Octagon House** (2645 Gough St. at Union
St.). It is one of the two remaining examples in
the city of this mid-19th-century architectural
form. The second landmark octagon is a private
residence on Russian Hill. These two curious
houses are all that is left locally of a national fad
for eight-sided buildings that swept the country
during the 1850s, inspired by a book written by
a New York phrenologist, Orson S. Fowler.
Eight-sided homes were thought to be good
luck.

In 1953 the National Society of the Colony
Dames of America purchased the Octagon
House (built in 1861) for one dollar from the Pacific Gas & Electric Company. One condition
stated that the structure had to be moved from
its original site across the street at 2648 Gough
Street. Today it serves as a museum and center

for the society's activities. The house is a treasure trove of American antique furniture and accessories from the 18th and 19th centuries. *Admission free. Open 2nd Sun. and 2nd and 4th Thurs. of each month noon–3.*

Union Street is a popular browsing ground. Here are some local favorites: The wild yet elegant contemporary art furniture at **Arte Forma** (1775 Union St.) includes multicolored leather sofas and eerie rice-paper lamps by Noguchi. **Images of the North** (1782 Union St.) specializes in superb Inuit art from Alaska and Canada.

Laura Ashley (1827 Union St.) brings a touch of Edwardian elegance to the street. Down the way, the epoch switches to Victorian, where naughty-but-nice romantic lingerie lies behind the quaint doors of **Victoria's Secret** (2245 Union St.)

If you like country furnishings, be sure to view the pre-1935 American quilt collection at **Yankee Doodle Dandy** (1974 Union St.). Delight a youngster with a charming stuffed animal made of vintage quilt bits.

Time Out   On the 1900 block are two special eating spots. Try **Bepples** (1934 Union St.) for a fabulous pie-and-coffee break. **Perry's** (1944 Union St.) has long had a reputation as the singles bar and the crowds still flock here to see and be seen. It's also a popular all-day drop-in restaurant, and it serves a tasty hamburger.

⑥③ The so-called **Wedding Houses** at 1980 Union Street were built during the late-1870s or 1880s. The romantic history of No. 1980 recounts that its builder, a dairy farmer named James Cudworth, sold the property to a father as wedding presents for his two daughters. In 1963 this property and the adjoining buildings were tastefully transformed from modest residences into charming flower-decked shops and cafés. Join some of San Francisco's young, rich, and trendy at **Prego** (2000 Union St.) and check out the latest in food and finery.

⑥④ Meander west to Webster Street, make a right, and continue down to the old **Vedanta Temple** (2963 Webster St.) at the corner of Filbert

Street. This 1905 architectural cocktail may be
the most unusual structure in San Francisco:
It's a pastiche of Colonial, Queen Anne, Moorish, and Hindu opulence. Vedanta is the highest
of the six Hindu systems of religious philosophy.
One of its basic tenets is that all religions are
paths to one goal.

If you care to check out still more fashionable
shops, return to Union Street and continue on to
Fillmore Street. Stroll north down Fillmore to
Greenwich Street, where a number of small,
fascinating shops have recently opened their doors. Two of the city's top dealers of Oriental art
have settled here. On the corner is one of the
city's most popular moderately priced restaurants, the casual, always-crowded **Balboa Café**.

Tour 11: Pacific Heights

Pacific Heights forms an east–west ridge along
the city's northern flank from Van Ness Avenue
to the Presidio and from California Street to the
bay. Some of the city's most expensive and dramatic real estate, including mansions and town
houses priced at $1 million and up, are located
here. Grand old Victorians, expensively face-
lifted, grace tree-lined streets, although here
and there glossy, glass-walled condo high rises
obstruct the view.

Old money and some new, trade and diplomatic
personnel, personalities in the limelight, and
those who prefer absolute media anonymity occupy the city's most prestigious residential enclave. Receptions at the Gorden Getty mansion
can block Broadway traffic while irate demon-
strators picket the Soviet Consulate on Green
Street. Rolls-Royces, Mercedes, and security
systems are commonplace.

Few visitors see anything other than the pleas
ing facades of Queen Anne charmers, English
Tudor imports, and Baroque bastions, but
strolling can still be a jackpot. The area encompasses a variety of great and small private
homes. Many of the structures stand close together but extend in a vertical direction for two
or more stories. A distinguishing feature of
some of the grand residences is an ornate gate.

A good place to begin a tour of the neighborhood is at the corner of Webster Street and Pacific Avenue, deep in the heart of the Heights. You can get here from Union Square by taking Muni bus No. 3 from Sutter and Stockton to Jackson and Fillmore streets. Turn right and walk one block east to Webster Street.

North on Webster Street, at 2550, is the massive Georgian brick mansion built in 1896 for William B. Bourn, who had inherited a Mother Lode gold mine. The architect, Willis Polk, was responsible for many of the most traditional and impressive commercial and private homes built from the prequake days until the early 1920s. (Be sure to see his 1917 Hallidie Building, 130 Sutter Street; *see* Tour 2: The Financial District, *above*.)

Neighbors include a consulate and, on the northwest corner, two classic showplaces. **2222 Broadway** is the three-story Italian Renaissance palace built by Comstock mine heir James Flood. Broadway uptown, unlike its North Beach stretch, is big league socially. The former Flood residence was given to a religious order. Ten years later, the Convent of the Sacred Heart purchased the Baroque brick **Grant house** (2220 Broadway) and both serve as school quarters today. A second top-drawer school, the **Hamlin** (2120 Broadway), occupies another Flood property.

Go east on Broadway and at the next corner turn right onto Buchanan Street and continue south to 2090 Jackson Street. The massive red sandstone **Whittier Mansion** was one of the most elegant 19th-century houses in the state, built so solidly that only a chimney toppled over during the 1906 earthquake. Next door at 2099 Pacific Avenue, is the North Baker Library of the California Historical Society. The library houses a fine collection of local historical documents but is only open to researchers and has no public displays.

Proceed east another block to **Laguna Street**. The Italianate Victorians on the east side of the 1800 block of Laguna Street cost only $2,000–$2,600 when they were built during the 1870s.

This block is one of the most photographed rows of Victorians in the city.

One block south, at Washington Street, is **⑥⑥ Lafayette Park,** a four-block-square oasis for sunbathers and dog-and-Frisbee teams. During the 1860s a tenacious squatter, Sam Holladay, built himself a big house of wood shipped round the Horn, in the center of the park. Holladay even instructed city gardeners as if the land were his own, and defied all attempts to remove him. The house was finally torn down in 1936.

The most imposing residence is the formal French **Spreckels Palace** (2080 Washington St.). Sugar heir Adolph Spreckels's wife was so pleased that she commissioned architect George Applegarth to design the city's European museum, the California Palace of the Legion of Honor in Lincoln Park.

Continue south on Gough Street (pronounced "Goff"), which runs along the east side of the park. A number of Queen Anne Victorians here have been lovingly restored. Two blocks south and one east, at the corner of California and Franklin, is an impressive twin-turreted Queen Anne–style Victorian built for a Gold Rush mining and lumber baron. North on Franklin Street, at 1735, stands a stately brick Georgian, built during the early 1900s for a coffee merchant.

⑥⑦ At 2007 Franklin is the handsome **Haas-Lilienthal Victorian.** Built in 1886, at an original cost of $20,000, this grand Queen Anne survived the 1906 earthquake and fire, and is the only fully furnished Victorian open to the public. The carefully kept rooms offer an intriguing glimpse into turn-of-the-century taste and lifestyle. A small display of photographs on the bottom floor proves that this elaborate house was modest compared with some of the giants that fell to the fire. It is operated by the Foundation for San Francisco's Architectural Heritage, and tours are given by docent volunteers. *Tel. 415/441–3004. Admission: $4 adults, $2 senior citizens and children under 12. Open Wed. noon–4, Sun. 11–4:30.*

By the mid-1970s, dozens of San Francisco's shabby gingerbreads were sporting psychedelic-colored facades, and the trend continues. Renovated treasures are found not only in the Haight-Ashbury district but increasingly in the Western Addition as well as in the working-class Mission area.

Tour 12: Japantown

Japanese-Americans began gravitating to the neighborhood known as the Western Addition prior to the 1906 earthquake. Early immigrants arrived about 1860, and they named San Francisco Soko. After the 1906 fire had destroyed wooden homes in other parts of the stricken city, many survivors settled in the Western Addition. By the 1930s the pioneers had opened shops, markets, meeting halls, and restaurants and established Shinto and Buddhist temples. Japantown was virtually disbanded during World War II when many of its residents, including second- and third-generation Americans, were "relocated" in camps.

Today **Japantown**, or "Nihonmachi," is centered on the slopes of Pacific Heights, north of Geary Boulevard, between Fillmore and Laguna streets. The Nihonmachi Cherry Blossom Festival is celebrated two weekends every April with a calendar of ethnic events. Walking in Nihonmachi is more than just a shopping and culinary treat; it is a cultural, sensory experience.

To reach Japantown from Union Square, take the Muni bus No. 38-Geary or No. 2, 3, or 4 on Sutter Street, westbound to Laguna. Remember to have exact change—fare is 85¢; free transfers are good for one direction and one change of vehicles.

We recommend visiting Japantown and the Western Addition during the day. Though the hotel, restaurant, and Kabuki movie complex are relatively safe in the evenings, it is often difficult to avoid long waits at isolated bus stops or to find a cruising cab when you want to get back to the hotel. The proximity of the often-hostile street gangs in the Western Addition could cause unpleasant incidents.

The buildings around the traffic-free **Japan Center Mall** between Sutter and Post streets are of the shoji screen school of architecture, and Ruth Asawa's origami fountain sits in the middle. (*See* Tour 1: Union Square, *above,* for more information on Ms. Asawa.) The mall faces the three-block-long, five-acre **Japan Center.** In 1968 the multimillion-dollar development created by noted American architect Minoru Yamasaki opened with a three-day folk festival. The three-block cluster includes an 800-car public garage and shops and showrooms selling Japanese products: electronic products, cameras, tapes and records, porcelains, pearls, and paintings.

The center is dominated by its Peace Plaza and Pagoda located between the East and Kintetsu buildings. Designed by Professor Yoshiro Taniguchi of Tokyo, an authority on ancient Japanese buildings, the plaza is landscaped with traditional Japanese-style gardens and reflecting pools. A graceful *yagura* (wooden drum tower) spans the entrance to the plaza and the copper-roofed *Heiwa Dori* (Peace Walkway) at the north end connects the East and Kintetsu buildings. The five-tiered, 100-foot Peace Pagoda overlooks the plaza, where seasonal festivals are held. The pagoda draws on the tradition of miniature round pagodas dedicated to eternal peace by Empress Koken in Nara more than 1,200 years ago. It was designed by the Japanese architect Yoshiro Taniguchi "to convey the friendship and goodwill of the Japanese to the people of the United States." A cultural bridge modeled after Florence's Ponte Vecchio spans Webster Street.

Soko Hardware (1698 Post St.) has been run by the Ashizawa merchant family since 1925. They specialize in beautifully crafted Japanese tools for gardening and carpentry. Visitors interested in Japanese cuisine might purchase seeds of Japanese vegetables to plant at home. They also have those long-sleeved, back-fastening Japanese aprons.

Nichi Bei Bussan (1715 Buchanan St.), in business since 1907, has a collector's choice of quilts covered with fabulous Japanese designs. They are stocked in twin and regular sizes; king-size quilts can be special-ordered. Prices start at about $75. Charming baby's **chan-chan-ko** (tiny printed Japanese-style vests) are popular gifts. Refrigerator door magnets in sushi motifs make super stocking stuffers.

Kinokuniya, on the second floor of the West Building, may have the finest selection of English-language books on Japanese subjects in the United States. There are books on food, *ikebana* (the art of flower arranging), handsomely bound editions of Japanese philosophy, religion, literature, and art, plus a large selection of elegant art calendars.

Also on the second floor is **Shige Antiques**, where collectors of art-to-wear search for antique hand-painted silk-embroidered kimonos and the all-important waist sash—the *obi*. The methods of tying the obi indicate the wearer's age, marital status, and even the special events being attended, such as weddings and funerals. The Arita porcelains, silk calligraphy scrolls, tea-ceremony utensils, and treasured lacquerware boxes at Shige will dazzle aficionados.

Asakichi, on the first floor of the West Building, specializes in antique blue-and-white Imari porcelains and handsome *tansu* (chests).

The shops in the East Building are a paradise for souvenir shoppers. Colorful flying-fish kites and delicate floral-patterned cocktail napkins are popular choices.

Some 40 restaurants in the neighborhood feature a choice of Japanese, Chinese, or Korean food. Most are found in the mall, a few are on side streets, and the rest are in the center itself, concentrated on the "street of restaurants" in the West Building. Following the practice in Japan, plastic replicas of the various dishes are on view.

If touring has about done you in, we suggest a brief respite at the **Kabuki Hot Springs** (1750 Geary Blvd.). Open daily, the communal bath is open for men only on Monday, Tuesday, Thursday, and Saturday, and for women only on Wednesday, Friday, and Sunday. The spa offers a number of steam, sauna, and massage packages. One, the Shogun, includes an hour of shiatsu massage. This method concentrates on pressure points in the body and is guaranteed to get you back on the track.

Time Out At a sushi bar, sample the bite-size portions of lightly seasoned rice and seaweed topped with various kinds of seafood, usually raw. Try to manage the chopsticks, dip (don't drench) your portion into the soy sauce, and experience this typical Japanese favorite. Tea, sake, or excellent Japanese beer accompanies these morsels. One warning—the final bill is calculated by portion, and it is not unusual to run up a $20 tab per person. **Isobune,** in the Kentetsu Mall in Japan Center (tel. 415/563–1030), is unusual. The sushi chef prepares a variety of sushi, placing each small portion on a small wooden boat that floats on a "river" of water that circles the counter. The customer then fishes out a sampling. An inexpensive and popular snack are ramen (noodle dishes). The noodles are either boiled and served in a broth or prepared toss-fried with bits of greens and meat added for flavor. **Mifune,** also in the Kintetsu Mall, serves both hot and cold noodles as well as either the fat strands of udon noodles or the buckwheat soba.

Walk back east on Geary Boulevard to Gough Street. This enclave of expensive high-rise residential towers is known as Cathedral Hill. The ⑥⑨ dramatic **St. Mary's Cathedral** was dedicated in 1971 at a cost of $7 million. The impressive Catholic cathedral seats 2,500 people around the central altar. Above the altar is a spectacular cascade made of 7,000 aluminum ribs. Four magnificent stained-glass windows in the dome represent the four elements: the blue north window, water; the light-colored south window, the sun; the red west window, fire; and the green east window, earth. Designed by a team of local architects and Pier Nervi of Rome, the Italian travertine church is approached through spacious plazas.

Tour 13: Civic Center

San Francisco's Civic Center stands as one of the country's great city, state, and federal building complexes with handsome adjoining cultural institutions. It's the realization of the theories of turn-of-the-century proponents of the "City Beautiful."

(70) Facing Polk Street, between Grove and McAllister streets, **City Hall** is a Baroque masterpiece of granite and marble, modeled after the Capitol in Washington. Its dome is even higher than the Washington version, and it dominates the area. In front of the building are formal gardens with fountains, walkways, and seasonal flower beds. Brooks Exhibit Hall was constructed under this plaza in 1958 to add space for the frequent trade shows and other events based in the Civic Auditorium on Grove Street.

San Francisco's increasing numbers of homeless people are often seen in the city's green spaces. Visitors and residents should be aware of possible danger in strolling in park areas and deserted business sectors after dark.

(71) Across the plaza from City Hall on Larkin Street is the main branch of the **San Francisco Public Library.** (A new library is being built around the corner; when the library is completed in 1995 this site will become the new Asian Art Museum.) History buffs should visit the San Francisco History Room and Archives on the third floor. Historic photographs, maps, and other memorabilia are carefully documented for the layman or research scholar. *Tel. 415/557–4567. Open Tues., Fri. 12–6; Wed. 1–6; Thurs., Sat. 10–6.*

On the west side of City Hall, across Van Ness Avenue, are the Museum of Modern Art, the Opera House, and Davies Symphony Hall. The northernmost of the three is the Veterans' Building, whose third and fourth floors house **(72)** the **Museum of Modern Art.** (A new MOMA is under construction as part of the downtown Yerba Buena development.) The museum's permanent collection was significantly enhanced in 1991 by the $40 million Haas bequest, which features Matisse's masterpiece, *Woman in a Hat,* as well as works by Derain, Manet, Monet, and Picasso. Traveling exhibitions bring important national and international paintings, photographs, graphics, and sculpture to the Bay Area. The

Museum Store has a select offering of books, posters, cards, and crafts. The Museum Cafe serves light snacks as well as wine and beer. *At McAllister St. and Van Ness Ave., tel. 415/863–8800. Admission: $4 adults, $2 senior citizens and students 13 and over with ID; free 1st Tues. of the month. Open Tues., Wed., Fri. 10–5; Thurs. 10–9, weekends 11–5. Closed major holidays.*

73 South of the Veteran's Building is the opulent **War Memorial Opera House,** which opened in 1932. Lotfi Mansouri has taken over as head of the San Francisco Opera, the largest opera company west of New York. Its regular season of world-class productions runs from September through December.

74 South of Grove Street, still on Van Ness Avenue, is the $27.5 million home of the San Francisco Symphony, the modern 3,000-plus-seat **Louise M. Davies Symphony Hall,** made of glass and granite. *Grove St. and Van Ness Ave., tel. 415/552–8338. Cost: $3 adults, $2 senior citizens and students. Tours of Davies Hall Wed. 1:30, 2:30, Sat. 12:30, 1:30. Tours of Davies Hall and the adjacent Performing Arts Center every ½ hour Mon. 10–2:30.*

The San Francisco Opera Shop, up the street from Davies Hall, carries books, T-shirts, posters, and gift items associated with the performing arts. *199 Grove St., tel. 415/565–6414. Open Mon. 11–5, Tues.–Fri. 11–6, Sat. noon–6, Sun. noon–6 during matinees. (It frequently stays open till 8:30 during performances of the Opera and Symphony.)*

75 East of the Civic Center at Market and Fulton streets, the **United Nations Plaza** is the site of a bustling farmers' market on Wednesday and Sunday.

Time Out　There are at least 40 restaurants within walking distance of the Civic Center. **Max's,** at 601 Van Ness Avenue in Opera Plaza, an upscale condo complex, serves such old-time favorites as lox and bagels and roast beef sandwiches as well as chicken Oriental salad, tortilla snacks, and tasty desserts. Don't be in a hurry: Service tends to be slow, especially on show nights (opera or symphony). Celebrity chef Jeremiah Tower's **Stars** (170 Redwood Alley, near Grove St. and Van Ness Ave.) offers exotic versions of California cuisine in an atmospheric room reminiscent of a Parisian bistro. For a quick pizza or a grilled chicken breast sandwich, dash across to **Spuntino** (524 Van Ness Ave.). Open until midnight on Friday and Saturday, this is an excellent spot for an after-theater cappuccino. No reservations or credit cards.

Tour 14: The Northern Waterfront

Numbers in the margin correspond to points of interest on the Northern Waterfront map.

For the sight, sound, and smell of the sea, hop the Powell-Hyde cable car from Union Square to the end of the line. From the cable car turnaround, Aquatic Park and the National Maritime Museum are immediately to the west; Fort Mason, with its several interesting museums, is just a bit farther west. If you're interested in exploring the more commercial attractions, Ghirardelli Square is behind you and Fisherman's Wharf to the east. We recommend casual clothes, good walking shoes, and a jacket or sweater for mid-afternoon breezes or foggy mists.

Or you could begin your day with one of the early-morning boat tours that depart from the Northern Waterfront piers. On a clear day (almost always), the morning light casts a warm glow on the colorful homes on Russian Hill, the weather-aged fishing boats cluttered at Fisherman's Wharf, rosy Ghirardelli Square and its fairy-tale clock tower, and the swelling seas beyond the entrance to the bay.

San Francisco is famous for the arts and crafts that flourish on the streets. Each day more than 200 of the city's innovative jewelers, painters, potters, photographers, and leather workers offer their wares for sale. You'll find them at Fisherman's Wharf, Union Square, Embarcadero Plaza, and Cliff House. Be wary: Some of the items are from Mexican or other foreign factories, and some may be overpriced. If you can't live without the item, try to bargain.

❶ The **National Maritime Museum** exhibits ship models, photographs, maps, and other artifacts chronicling the development of San Francisco and the West Coast through maritime history. *Aquatic Park, at the foot of Polk St., tel. 415/ 556–8177. Admission free. Open daily 10–5, till 6 in summer.*

❷ The museum also includes the **Hyde Street Pier** (two blocks east), where historic vessels are moored. The highlight is the *Balclutha*, an 1886 full-rigged, three-mast sailing vessel that sailed around Cape Horn 17 times. The *Eureka*, a side-wheel ferry, and the *C.A. Thayer*, a three-masted schooner, can also be boarded. *Tel. 415/ 556–6435. Admission: $3 adults, children and senior citizens free. Open daily 10–5, 10–6 in summer.*

The *Pampanito*, at Pier 45, is a World War II submarine. An audio tour has been installed. *Tel. 415/929–0202. Admission: $4 adults; $2 students 12–18; $1 children 6–11, senior citizens, and active military. Open Sun.–Thurs. 9–6, Fri.–Sat. 9–9, daily 9–9 in summer.*

❸ **Fort Mason,** originally a depot for the shipment of supplies to the Pacific during World War II, was converted into a cultural center in 1977. The immense, three-story, yellow-stucco buildings are nondescript. Four minimuseums and an outstanding vegetarian restaurant merit mention, however.

The **Mexican Museum** was the first American showcase to be devoted exclusively to Mexican and Mexican-American art. Plans are underway to build a larger modern building for the museum in the downtown Yerba Buena complex by the mid-1990s. The museum's goal is to expose the vitality and scope of Mexican art from pre-Hispanic Indian terra-cotta figures and Spanish Colonial religious images to modern Mexican masters. Limited space allows only a fraction of the permanent collection, including a recent 500-piece folk-art collection (a gift from the Nelson A. Rockefeller estate), to be exhibited. The museum recently began mounting major special shows. One of the early, very successful exhibits displayed the work of Frida Kahlo, the Mexican

Northern Waterfront: Tours 14–15

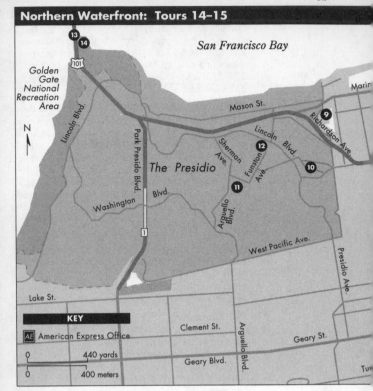

San Francisco Bay

Golden Gate National Recreation Area

The Presidio

KEY

AE American Express Office

| 0 | 440 yards |
| 0 | 400 meters |

Buena Vista Cafe, **6**
The Cannery, **5**
Fisherman's Wharf, **7**
Fort Mason, **3**
Fort Point, **14**

Ghirardelli Square, **4**
Golden Gate Bridge, **13**
Hyde Street Pier, **2**
National Maritime Museum, **1**

Officers' Club, **11**
Palace of Fine Arts, **9**
Pier 39, **8**
Presidio, **10**
Presidio Army Museum, **12**

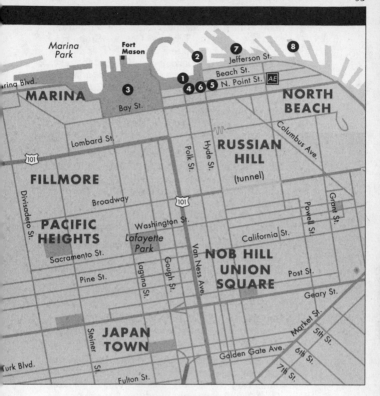

surrealist and wife of Diego Rivera. The permanent collection includes such contemporary greats as Rivera, Tamayo, Orozco, Siquieros, and sculptor Francisco Zuniga. La Tienda, the museum shop, stocks colorful Mexican folk art, posters, books, and catalogues from museum exhibitions. *Fort Mason, Bldg. D., tel. 415/441–0404. Free admission on the 1st Wed. of the month. Admission: $3 adults, $2 senior citizens and students, children under 10 free. Open Wed.–Sun. noon–5.*

The **Museo Italo Americano** has permanent exhibits of works of 19th- and 20th-century Italian-American artists. Shows include paintings, sculpture, etchings, and photographs. The museum presents special exhibits, lectures, and films. *Fort Mason, Bldg. C, tel. 415/673–2200. Admission free. Open Wed.–Sun. noon–5.*

The **San Francisco African-American Historical and Cultural Society** maintains the only black museum west of the Rockies. The permanent collection includes exhibits on black California and black Civil War history. Temporary exhibits focus on living California black artists. *Fort Mason, Bldg. C, Room 165, tel. 415/441–0640. Admission: donation. Open Wed.–Sun. noon–5. We suggest you phone to verify schedules.*

The **San Francisco Crafts and Folk Art Museum** features American folk art, tribal art, and contemporary crafts. *Fort Mason, Bldg. A, tel. 415/ 775–0990. Admission: $1 adults, 50¢ senior citizens and children; admission free Sat. 10– noon. Open Tues.–Sun. 11–5, Sat. 10–5.*

Several theater companies are housed at Fort Mason. Of particular note is the **Magic Theatre** (Fort Mason, Bldg. D, tel. 415/441–8822), known for producing the works of such contemporary playwrights as Sam Shepard and Michael McClure.

The SS *Jeremiah O'Brien* is a World War II Liberty Ship freighter. The ship is staffed by volunteers, and there are special "steaming weekends," when the steam engine is in operation, the coal stove galley is open, and the "Slop Chest" store is set up. This is usually the third weekend of the month, but call to verify. *Fort*

Mason, Pier 3 East, Marina Blvd. and Buchanan St., tel. 415/441–3101. Admission: $2 adults,
$1 children and senior citizens, $5 per family.
Admission on steaming weekends: $3 adults, $1
children and senior citizens, $6 per family.
Open weekdays 9–3, weekends 9–4.

Time Out The San Francisco Zen Center operates a famous and beautiful restaurant at Fort Mason.
Greens (Fort Mason, Bldg. A, tel. 415/771–6222)
has won international acclaim for its innovative
vegetarian menu. The room is decorated with
contemporary art and offers some of the finest
views (from down close to the water) across the
bay to the Golden Gate Bridge. Reservations
are essential, but you can stop by the bakery
during the day and pick up some of their famous
bread and pastries.

④ Spend some time strolling through **Ghirardelli
Square,** which is across Beach Street from the
National Maritime Museum. This charming
complex of 19th-century brick factory buildings
has been transformed into specialty shops,
cafés, restaurants, and galleries. Until the early
1960s, the Ghirardelli Chocolate Company's
aromatic production perfumed the Northern
Waterfront. Two unusual shops deserve mention: **Light Opera** specializes in exquisite Russian lacquer boxes. (**Gump's** on Post Street also
shows these sophisticated treasures, priced
from about $50 to $20,000.) **Xanadu Gallery** displays museum-quality tribal art from Asia, Africa, Oceania, and the Americas. Their array of
antique and ethnic jewelry is peerless.

⑤ Just east of the Hyde Street Pier, **The Cannery**
is a three-story structure built in 1894 to house
the Del Monte Fruit and Vegetable Cannery.
Shops, art galleries, and unusual restaurants
ring the courtyard today, and the new **Museum
of the City of San Francisco** can be found on the
third floor. The first independent museum on
the history of the city displays a number of significant historical items, maps, and photographs, including the eight-ton head of the
Goddess of Progress statue that toppled from
City Hall just before the 1906 earthquake. *2801*

Leavenworth St., tel. 415/928–0289. Admission free. Open Wed.–Sun. 11–4.

Just across the street, additional shopping and snacking choices are offered at the flag-festooned **Anchorage mall**.

6 The mellow **Buena Vista Cafe** (2765 Hyde St.) claims to be the birthplace of Irish Coffee stateside; the late San Francisco columnist Stan Delaplane is credited with importing the Gaelic concoction. The BV opens at 9 AM, serving a great breakfast. It is always crowded; try for a table overlooking nostalgic Victorian Park with its cable-car turntable.

7 A bit farther down at Taylor and Jefferson streets is **Fisherman's Wharf**. Numerous seafood restaurants are located here, as well as sidewalk crab pots and counters that offer takeaway shrimp and crab cocktails. Ships creak at their moorings; sea gulls cry out for a handout. By mid-afternoon, the fishing fleet is back to port. T-shirts and sweats, gold chains galore, redwood furniture, acres of artwork—some original—beckon visitors. Wax museums, fastfood favorites, amusing street artists, and the animated robots at Lazer Maze provide diversions for all ages.

Time Out A great family spot on the wharf is **Bobby Rubino's** (245 Jefferson St.). Barbecued ribs, shrimp, chicken, and burgers—there is something tasty for everyone. A favorite with couples is crowded, noisy **Houlihan's** at the Anchorage mall. It is noted for fancy drinks, fantastic bay views, tasty pizza and pastas, plus nightly music and dancing.

Today's tourists daily have the opportunity of enjoying exhilarating cruising on the bay. Among the cruises of the **Red and White Fleet**, berthed at Pier 41, are frequent 45-minute swings under the Golden Gate Bridge and the Northern Waterfront. Advanced reservations are strongly recommended for the very popular Alcatraz Island tour, which enables passengers to take a self-guided tour through the prison and grounds. *Reservations for individuals from*

*Ticketron, Box 26430, 94126, tel. 415/546–2896.
Cost: $5; $8.50 with audio tour.*

The **Blue and Gold Fleet**, berthed at Pier 39,
provides its passengers with validated parking
across the street. The 1¼-hour tour sails under
both the Bay and Golden Gate bridges. Dinner-
dance cruises run April–mid-December. *Tel.
415/781–7877. Reservations not necessary. Bay
Cruise: $14 adults, $7 senior citizens and children 5–18, under 5 free. Summertime dinner-
dance cruise: $35 per person (group rates avail-
able). Daily departures.*

8 **Pier 39** is the most popular of San Francisco's
waterfront attractions, drawing millions of visitors each year to browse through its dozens of
shops. Check out The Disney Store, with more
Mickey Mouses than you can shake a stick at;
Left Hand World, where left-handers will find
all manner of gadgets designed with lefties in
mind; and Only in San Francisco, the place for
San Francisco memorabilia and the location of
the Pier 39 information center. The myriad
eateries confuse those seeking a traditional
soda-and-burger stop. Ongoing free entertainment, accessible validated parking, and nearby
public transportation ensure crowds most days.

Tour 15: The Marina and the Presidio

9 San Francisco's rosy and Rococo **Palace of Fine
Arts** is at the very end of the Marina, near the
intersection of Baker and Beach streets. The
palace is the sole survivor of the 32 tinted plaster structures built for the 1915 Panama-Pacific
Exposition. Bernard Maybeck designed the Roman Classic beauty, and legions of sentimental
citizens and a huge private donation saved the
palace. It was reconstructed in concrete at a
cost of $7 million and reopened in 1967. The mas-
sive columns, great rotunda, and swan-filled la-
goon will be familiar from fashion layouts as well
as many recent films. Recently, travelers on
package tours from Japan have been using it as a
backdrop for wedding-party photos, with the
brides wearing Western-style finery.

The interior houses a fascinating hands-on museum, the **Exploratorium**. It has been called the
best science museum in the world. The curious

of all ages flock here to try to use and understand some of the 600 exhibits. Be sure to include the pitch-black, crawl-through Tactile Dome in your visit. *Tel. 415/563-7337. Prices and hours subject to change, so call ahead. Admission: $7 adults, $3 children under 17. Reservations required for Tactile Dome.*

If you have a car, now is the time to use it for a drive through the **Presidio.** (If not, Muni bus No. 38 from Union Square will take you to Park Presidio; from there use a free transfer to bus No. 28 into the Presidio.) A military post for more than 200 years, this headquarters of the U.S. Sixth Army may soon become a public park. De Anza and a band of Spanish settlers claimed the area in 1776. It became a Mexican garrison in 1822 when Mexico gained its independence from Spain. U.S. troops forcibly occupied it in 1846.

The more than 1,500 acres of rolling hills, majestic woods, and attractive redbrick army barracks present an air of serenity in the middle of the city. There are two beaches, a golf course, and picnic sites. The **Officers' Club,** a long, low adobe, was the Spanish commandante's headquarters, built about 1776, and is the oldest standing building in the city. The **Presidio Army Museum** is housed in the former hospital and focuses on the role played by the military in San Francisco's development. *On the corner of Lincoln Blvd. and Funston Ave., tel. 415/561-4115. Admission free. Open Tues.–Sun. 10–4.*

Muni bus No. 28 will take you to the **Golden Gate Bridge** toll plaza. San Francisco celebrated the 50th birthday of the orange suspension bridge in 1987. Nearly 2 miles long, connecting San Francisco with Marin County, its Art Deco design is powerful, serene, and tough, made to withstand winds of over 100 miles per hour. Though frequently gusty and misty (walkers should wear warm clothing), the bridge offers unparalleled views of the Bay Area. The east walkway offers a glimpse of the San Francisco skyline as well as the islands of the bay. On a sunny day sailboats dot the water, and brave windsurfers test the often treacherous tides beneath the bridge. The view west confronts you with the wild hills of the Marin headlands, the curving coast south to Lands End, and the majestic Pacific Ocean. There's a vista point on the Marin side, where you can contemplate the city and its spectacular setting.

⑭ Fort Point was constructed during the years 1853–1861 to protect San Francisco from sea attack during the Civil War. It was designed to mount 126 cannons with a range of up to 2 miles. Standing under the shadow of the Golden Gate Bridge, the national historic site is now a museum filled with military memorabilia. Guided group tours are offered by National Park Rangers, and there are cannon demonstrations. There is a superb view of the bay from the top floor. *Tel. 415/556–1693. Admission free. Open daily 10–5.*

From here, hardy walkers may elect to stroll about 3½ miles (with bay views) along the Golden Gate Promenade to Aquatic Park and the Hyde Street cable car terminus.

Tour 16: Golden Gate Park

It was a Scotsman, John McLaren, who became manager of Golden Gate Park in 1887 and transformed the brush and sand into the green civilized wilderness we enjoy today. Here you can attend a polo game or a Sunday band concert and rent a bike, boat, or roller skates. On Sundays, some park roads are closed to cars and come alive with joggers, bicyclists, skaters, museum goers, and picnickers. There are tennis courts, baseball diamonds, soccer fields, and a buffalo paddock, and miles of trails for horseback riding in this 1,000-acre park.

Because it is so large, the best way for most visitors to see it is by car. Muni buses provide service, though on weekends there may be a long wait. On Market Street, board a west-bound No. 5-Fulton or No. 21-Hayes bus and continue to Arguello and Fulton streets. Walk south about 500 feet to John F. Kennedy Drive.

From May through October, free guided walking tours of the park are offered every weekend by the Friends of Recreation and Parks (tel. 415/221–1311).

The oldest building in the park and perhaps San Francisco's most elaborate Victorian is the **Conservatory**, a copy of London's famous Kew Gardens. The ornate greenhouse was originally brought around the Horn for the estate of James Lick in San Jose. The Conservatory was purchased from the Lick estate with public subscription funds and erected in the park. In addition to a tropical garden, there are seasonal displays of flowers and plants and a permanent exhibit of rare orchids.

The eastern section of the park has three museums. The **M.H. de Young Memorial Museum** was completely reorganized in 1989. It now features American art, with collections of painting, sculpture, textiles, and decorative arts from Colonial times through the 20th century. Fifteen new galleries highlight the work of American masters including Copley, Eakins, Bingham, and Sargent. Don't miss the room of landscapes, dominated by Frederic Church's moody, almost psychedelic Rainy Season in the Tropics. There is a wonderful gallery of American still-life and trompe l'oeil art and a small selection of classic Shaker furniture. The de Young has also retained its dramatic collection of tribal art from Africa, Oceania, and the Americas, which includes pottery, basketry, sculpture, and ritual clothing and accessories. In addition to its permanent collections, the museum hosts selected traveling shows—often blockbuster events for which there are long lines and additional admission charges.

The museum has an outstanding shop with a wide selection of art objects. The **Cafe de Young**, which has outdoor seating in the Oakes Garden, serves a complete menu of light refreshments until 4 PM. *Tel. 415/863-3330 for 24-hour information. Admission: $5 adults, $3 senior citizens, $2 youths 12-17, under 12 free. Free 1st Wed. and Sat. morning of the month. Note: One admission charge admits you to the de Young, Asian Art, and Legion of Honor museums on the same day. Open Wed.-Sun. 10-5.*

The **Asian Art Museum** is located in galleries that adjoin the de Young. This world-famous Avery Brundage collection consists of more than 10,000 sculptures, paintings, and ceramics that illustrate major periods of Asian art. Very special are the Magnin Jade Room and the Leventritt collection of blue and white porcelains. On the second floor are treasures from Iran, Turkey, Syria, India, Tibet, Nepal, Pakistan, Korea, Japan, Afghanistan, and Southeast Asia. Both the de Young and Asian Art museums have daily docent tours. *Tel. 415/668–8921. Admission collected when entering the de Young. Open Wed.–Sun. 10–5.*

Time Out The **Japanese Tea Garden,** next to the Asian Art Museum, is ideal for resting after museum touring. This charming four-acre village was created for the 1894 Mid-Winter Exposition. Small ponds, streams, and flowering shrubs create a serene landscape. The cherry blossoms in spring are exquisite. The Tea House (tea, of course, and cookies are served) is popular and busy. *Tel. 415/752–1171. Admission: $2 adults, $1 senior residents of San Francisco and children 6–12. Free 1st Wed. of each month. Open daily 8:30–6:30.*

The **California Academy of Sciences** is directly opposite the de Young Museum. It is one of the five top natural history museums in the country and has both an aquarium and a planetarium. Throngs of visitors enjoy its Steinhart Aquarium, with its dramatic 100,000-gallon Fish Roundabout, home to 14,000 creatures, and a living coral reef with colorful fish, giant clams, tropical sharks, and a rainbow of hard and soft corals. There is an additional charge for Morrison Planetarium shows ($2.50 adults, $1.25 senior citizens and students, tel. 415/750–7138 for daily schedule). The Space and Earth Hall has an "earthquake floor" that enables visitors to ride a simulated California earthquake. The Wattis Hall of Man presents lifelike habitat scenes that range from the icy terrain of the arctic Inuit to the lush highlands of New Guinea. Newly renovated is the Wild California Hall, with a 10,000-gallon aquarium tank showing underwater life at the Farallones (islands off the coast of northern California), life-size elephant seal models, and video information on the wildlife of the state. A stuffed great white shark, caught off the waters of Half Moon Bay, was added in 1989. The genuine 13½-foot, 1,500-pound "Jaws" is suspended in a tank. If you dare, you can look right into its gaping mouth. The innovative Life through Time Hall tells the story of evolution from the beginnings of the universe through the age of dinosaurs to the age of mammals. A cafeteria is open daily until one hour before the museum closes. The Academy Store offers a wide selection of books, posters, toys, and cultural artifacts. *Tel. 415/750-7145. Admission: $6 adults, $3 senior citizens and students 12-17, $1 children 6-11. $2 discount with Muni transfer. Free 1st Wed. of each month. Open daily July 4-Labor Day 10-7, Labor Day-July 3 10-5.*

A short stroll from the Academy of Sciences will take you to the free **Shakespeare Garden.** Two hundred flowers mentioned by the Bard, as well as bronze-engraved panels with floral quotations, are set throughout the garden.

Strybing Arboretum specializes in plants from areas with climates similar to that of the Bay Area, such as the west coast of Australia, South Africa, and the Mediterranean. There are many gardens inside the grounds, with 6,000 plants and tree varieties blooming seasonally. *9th Ave. at Lincoln Way, tel. 415/661-0668. Admission free. Open weekdays 8-4:30, weekends and holidays 10-5. Tours leave the bookstore weekdays at 1:30 PM, weekends at 10:30 AM and 1:30 PM.*

The western half of Golden Gate Park offers miles of wooded greenery and open spaces for all types of spectator and participant sports. Rent a paddleboat or stroll around **Stow Lake.** The Chinese Pavilion, a gift from the city of Taipei, was shipped in 6,000 pieces and assembled on the shore of Strawberry Hill Island in Stow Lake in 1981. At the very western end of the park, where Kennedy Drive meets the Great Highway, is the beautifully restored 1902 **Dutch Windmill** and the photogenic **Queen Wilhelmina Tulip Garden.**

Tour 17: Lincoln Park and the Western Shoreline

No other American city provides such close-up viewing of the power and fury of the surf attacking the shore. From Land's End in Lincoln Park you can look across the Golden Gate (the name was originally given to the opening of San Francisco Bay long before the bridge was built) to the Marin Headlands. From Cliff House south to the San Francisco Zoo, the Great Highway and Ocean Beach run along the western edge of the city.

The wind is often strong along the shoreline, summer fog can blanket the ocean beaches, and the water is cold and usually too rough for swimming. Carry a sweater or jacket and bring binoculars.

At the northwest corner of the San Francisco Peninsula is **Lincoln Park**. At one time all the city's cemeteries were here, segregated by nationality. Today there is an 18-hole golf course with large and well-formed Monterey cypresses lining the fairways. There are scenic walks throughout the 275-acre park, with particularly good views from **Land's End** (the parking lot is at the end of El Camino del Mar). The trails out to Land's End, however, are for skilled hikers only: There are frequent landslides, and danger lurks along the steep cliffs.

Also in Lincoln Park is the **California Palace of the Legion of Honor**. The building itself—modeled after the 18th-century Parisian original—is architecturally interesting and spectacularly situated on cliffs overlooking the ocean and the Golden Gate Bridge. The museum closed in 1992 for what is scheduled to be a two-year renovation, and is set to reopen in April 1994. In the meantime, the exterior is still worth a look.

Cliff House (1066 Point Lobos Ave.), where the road turns south along the western shore, has existed in several incarnations. The original, built in 1863, and several later structures were destroyed by fire. The present building has restaurants, a pub, and a gift shop. The lower dining room overlooks **Seal Rocks** (the barking marine mammals sunning themselves are actually sea lions).

An adjacent (free) attraction is the **Musée Mécanique**, a collection of antique mechanical contrivances, including peep shows and nickelodeons. The museum carries on the tradition of arcade amusement at the Cliff House. *Tel. 415/ 386–1170. Open weekdays 11–7, weekends 10–7.*

Two flights below Cliff House is a fine observation deck and the Golden Gate National Recreation Area **Visitors Center** (tel. 415/556–8642; open daily 10–4:30). There are interesting and historic photographs of Cliff House and the glass-roofed **Sutro Baths**. The baths covered three acres just north of Cliff House and comprised six enormous baths, 500 dressing rooms, and several restaurants. The baths were closed in 1952 and burned in 1966. You can explore the ruins on your own (the Visitors Center offers information on these and other trails) or take ranger-led walks on weekends.

Because traffic is often heavy in summer and on weekends, you might want to take the Muni system from the Union Square area out to Cliff House. On weekdays, take the Muni No. 38-Geary Limited to 48th Street and Point Lobos and walk down the hill. (On weekends and during the evenings, the Muni No. 38 is marked 48th Avenue.)

Time Out Cliff House has several restaurants and a busy bar. **The Upstairs Room** (tel. 415/387–5847) features a light menu with a number of omelet suggestions. The lower dining room, the **Terrace Room** (tel. 415/386–3330), has a fabulous view of Seal Rocks. Reservations are recommended, but you may still have to wait for a table, especially at midday on Sunday.

Below the Cliff House are the **Great Highway** and **Ocean Beach**. Stretching for 3 miles along the western (Pacific) side of the city, this is a beautiful beach for walking, running, or lying in the sun—but not for swimming. Although dozens of surfers head to Ocean Beach each day, you'll notice they are dressed head-to-toe in wetsuits, as the water here is extremely cold.

Across the highway from the beach is a new path, which winds through landscaped sand dunes from Lincoln Avenue to Sloat Boulevard (near the zoo)—an ideal route for walking and bicycling.

At the Great Highway and Sloat Boulevard is the **San Francisco Zoo**. The zoo was begun in 1889 in Golden Gate Park. At its present home there are 1,000 species of birds and animals, more than 130 of which have been designated endangered species. Among the protected are the snow leopard, Bengal tiger, red panda, jaguar, and the Asian elephant. One of the newest attractions is the greater one-horned rhino, next to the African elephants.

Gorilla World, a $2 million exhibit, is the largest and most natural gorilla habitat in a zoo. The circular outer area is carpeted with natural African Kikuyu grass, while trees, shrubs, and waterfalls create communal play areas. The $5 million Primate Discovery Center houses 16 endangered species in atriumlike enclosures. One of the most popular zoo residents is Prince Charles, a rare white tiger and the first of its kind to be exhibited in the West.

There are 33 "storyboxes" throughout the zoo that when turned on with the blue plastic elephant keys ($1.50) recite animal facts and basic zoological concepts in four languages (English, Spanish, Cantonese, and Tagalog).

The children's zoo has a minipopulation of about 300 mammals, birds, and reptiles, plus an insect zoo, a baby animal nursery, and a beautifully restored 1921 Dentzel Carousel. A ride astride one of the 52 hand-carved menagerie animals costs 75¢.

Zoo information, tel. 415/753–7083. Admission: $6 adults, $3 youths 12–15 and senior citizens, under 12 free when accompanied by an adult. Free 1st Wed. of the month. Open daily 10–5. Children's zoo admission: $1, under 3 free. Open daily 11–4.

Tour 18: The Mission District

Numbers in the margin correspond to points of interest on the Mission District and Castro Street map.

During the 19th century the sunny weather of the then-rural Mission District made it a popular locale for resorts, racetracks, and gambling places. At 13th and Mission streets, where freeway traffic now roars overhead, stood Woodward's Gardens, a lush botanical garden with a zoo, playground, and pavilions featuring acrobatic performances.

Mission Street is the commercial center of the district, and all the resident ethnic cultures are reflected in the businesses: Spanish-language theaters, Italian restaurants, Arab-owned clothing stores, Vietnamese markets, and Filipino, Hispanic, and Chinese restaurants and groceries. The majority of Latinos here are from Central America. Most of them settled here during the late 1960s and early 1970s; many of them are now service workers. The Mexican-Americans are a minority of the estimated 50,000 Hispanics in the Mission.

❶ **Mission Dolores,** on palm-lined Dolores Street, is the sixth of the 21 missions founded by Father Junipero Serra. The adobe building was begun in 1782 and was originally known as Mission San Francisco de Assisi. Completed in 1791, its ceiling depicts original Costanoan Indian basket designs, executed in vegetable dyes. There is a small museum, and the mission cemetery contains the graves of more than 5,000 Indians. *Dolores and 16th Sts., tel. 415/621–8203. Admission: $1. Open daily 9–4.*

❷ The nearby **Dolores Park** (Dolores St. between 18th and 20th Sts.) is a great picnic spot that offers dramatic views of the high rises of downtown as a backdrop for the pastel bay-windowed Mission District houses.

Two blocks from Mission Dolores, the area around 16th and Valencia streets is developing its own neighborhood character. A mix of socialists, lesbian-feminists, new wavers, and traditional Hispanics has made it San Francisco's

3 new bohemia. The **Roxie Theater** (3117 16th St.,
tel. 415/863–1087) is an aggressive showcase for
independent films. Across the street, **Cafe Pica-
ro** (3120 16th St.) appears to be a leftover from
the '60s. People gather here for political discus-
sions and to work on papers, read books, and
play chess while downing strong cappuccino and
hearty inexpensive meals.

4 The cornerstone of the women-owned and -run
businesses in the neighborhood is the **Women's
Building of the Bay Area** (3543 18th St., tel. 415/
431–1180), which for 10 years has held workshops and conferences of particular interest to
women. It houses offices for many social and political organizations and sponsors talks and
readings by such noted writers as Alice Walker
and Angela Davis. Bulletin boards announce
many women-oriented events in the Bay Area.

Time Out   You can eat better for less money in the Mission
District than anywhere else in the city. Stop in
at one of the *taquerias* (taco parlors), fast-food
eateries where the meals are nutritious and
very, very inexpensive. The staples are tacos
and burritos—but they are unlike those served
at Americanized fast-food places. At **La Cumbre**
(515 Valencia St., tel. 415/863–8205) and **El Toro**
(17th and Valencia Sts., tel. 415/431–3351), two
of the neighborhood's most popular taquerias,
the tacos are made with double-corn tortillas
piled high with a choice of meat and beans. And
the burritos are large, rolled-flour tortillas
stuffed with meat, rice, and beans. La Cumbre
is also well known for its *carne asada* (charcoal-
grilled steak); El Toro for its chicken simmered
in green chili sauce, and *carnitas* (crisp strips of
roast pork).

Colorful, crammed, noisy Mission Street may
represent the commercial artery of the Mission
District, but 24th Street is its heart. Here the
area takes on the flavor of another country, with
small open-air groceries selling huge Mexican
papayas and plantains, tiny restaurants serving
sopa de mariscos (fish soup), and an abundance
of religious shops and Latin bakeries. The feeling is more rural than on Mission Street and cer-
tainly less Anglo.

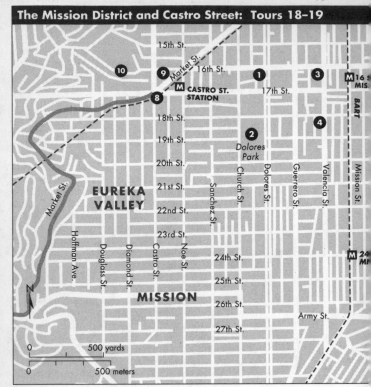

The Mission District and Castro Street: Tours 18–19

Balmy Alley, **6**

Castro
Theatre, **8**

Dolores Park, **2**

Galeria de la
Raza, **5**

Josephine D.
Randall Junior
Museum, **10**

Mission
Dolores, **1**

The Names
Project, **9**

Precita Eyes and
Ears Arts
Center, **7**

Roxie Theater, **3**

Women's
Building of the
Bay Area, **4**

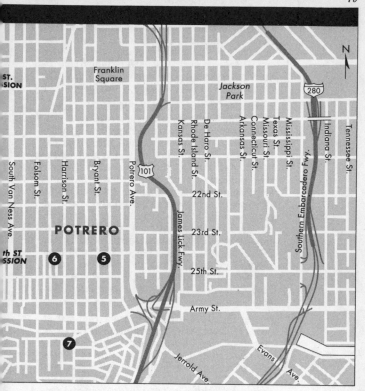

ST.
SION

Franklin
Square

Jackson
Park

280

Tennessee St.

Indiana St.

Southern Embarcadero Fwy.

Mississippi St.

Texas St.

Missouri St.

Connecticut St.

Arkansas St.

De Haro St.

Rhode Island St.

Kansas St.

101

Potrero Ave.

James Lick Fwy.

22nd St.

23rd St.

25th St.

Army St.

Evans Ave.

Jerrold Ave.

South Van Ness Ave.

Folsom St.

Harrison St.

Bryant St.

POTRERO

th ST
SION

6   5

7

N

⑤ Galeria de la Raza, at the east end of the street, is an important showcase for Hispanic art. It shows local and international artists, sometimes mounting events in conjunction with the Mexican Museum at Fort Mason. (A Frieda Kahlo exhibit in 1988 used both venues.) *2855 24th St., tel. 415/826–8009. Open Tues.–Sat. noon–6.*

Next door to the Gallery is Studio 24 Galeria Shop, which sells folklore handicrafts from Latin America. The studio specializes in figurines from *Dia de los Muertos*, the Latin American Halloween. The polychrome plaster skeletons—posed as if singing, dancing, or working—represent deceased family members come back for a visit, doing the kinds of things they did in life. The clay groupings can be quite elaborate, using such settings as cars, couches, and kitchens. The aim is to make death more familiar and less threatening; don't be surprised to see a skeleton calmly doing her ironing. Also look for the marvelously detailed Peruvian tapestries called *arpedas*, which also highlight daily life. *2857 24th St., tel. 415/826–8009. Open Tues.–Sat. noon–6.*

Art in the Mission District is not confined indoors. Keeping alive the tradition of the great muralist Diego Rivera, community artists have transformed the walls of their neighborhood **⑥** with paintings. In small **Balmy Alley** (between Treat and Harrison Sts. just off 24th St.), paint changes a funky side street into a dramatic aisle of color and purpose. The murals up and down the alley were begun in 1973 by a group of local children and continued by an affiliation of several dozen artists and community workers to pro- **⑦** mote peace in Central America. The **Precita Eyes and Ears Arts Center** gives guided walks of the Mission District's murals. The tour starts with a ½-hour slide presentation, and the walk takes about an hour, visiting over 40 murals in the area. *348 Precita Ave., tel. 415/285–2287. Tours every weekend, 1:30 PM. $3 adults, $1 students under 18. Walks can also be arranged by appointment for groups of 10 or more.*

Bakeries, or *panaderias*, are an essential stop on 24th Street. Don't expect light, buttery, flaky creations; Latin American pastries are strictly down-to-earth—but delicious. Try the Salvadorean specialty, *quesadillas*, which have cheese ground in with the flour and taste like sweet corn muffins; or *cemitas*, cake squares filled with pineapple. You take what looks good, with tongs and a tray provided at the counter. **La Victoria** (2937 24th St.) and **Dominguez** (2951 24th St.) on competing sides of the street are two of the best.

The **St. Francis Candy Store** (2801 24th St.) is a genuine soda fountain and ice-cream parlor that makes its own confections. An anomaly in the neighborhood, it looks like something from a Norman Rockwell painting.

Time Out　The Salvadorean restaurants that have opened in the Mission District during the past several years are great eating places. Their fare is a variation of traditional Mexican cooking that offers more stews and sauces. **El Tazumal** (3522 20th St., tel. 415/550–0935), off Mission Street at 20th Street, was one of the pioneers and has excellent, inexpensive lunches and dinners. Try the appetizers called *pupusas* (baked pancakes filled with ground meat or cheese) and the pork *chile verde* (cubes of meat simmered to succulence in a mild green chili/tomatillo sauce).

The Mission District plays fiesta for two important occasions. There is a weekend of festivities around the *cinco de Mayo* (5th of May) holiday, but the neighborhood really erupts into celebration on a sunny weekend in late spring called *carnaval*. This Rio-like three-day extravaganza gets larger each year. Recent festivities closed Harrison Street between 16th and 20th streets, with four stages for live music and dancers, as well as crafts and food booths. A Grand Carnaval Parade along 24th Street caps the celebration.

Tour 19: Castro Street

Starting during the early 1970s, the neighborhood around Castro Street became known for one of the most remarkable urban migrations in American history: the mass arrival of gay men and women in San Francisco, from all over the United States. What had been for decades a sunny, sedate, middle-class neighborhood of mostly Irish and Scandinavian families became a new colony that was either a gay ghetto or, as many thought, Gay Mecca.

Historians are still trying to discover what brought an estimated 100,000 to 250,000 gays and lesbians into the San Francisco area. Some point to the libertine tradition rooted in Barbary Coast piracy, prostitution, and gambling. Others note that as a huge military embarcation point during World War II, the city was occupied by tens of thousands of mostly single men. Whatever the cause, San Francisco became the city of choice for lesbians and gay men, and Castro Street, nestled at the base of Twin Peaks and just over Buena Vista hill from Haight Street, became its social, cultural, and political center.

From Powell Street, take the Muni Metro underground (trains K, L, M, or O) direct to the Castro Street station. You will come out into **Harvey Milk Plaza,** named for the man who electrified the city in 1977 by being voted onto the metropolitan board of supervisors as an openly gay candidate. The proprietor of a Castro Street camera store, Harvey Milk proved that the gay community of San Francisco was a political as well as a social force. His high visibility accompanied demands by homosexuals for thorough inclusion in the city's life—its power structures, not just its disco parties. San Francisco has responded with a tolerance found nowhere else in the United States: Gay people sit as municipal judges, police commissioners, and arts administrators.

Two events, though, have changed the tenor of the community. On November 27, 1978, barely a year after being elected, Harvey Milk and the liberal mayor George Moscone were assassinated by a disturbed member of the board of supervisors, Dan White. A few years later gay men began to awaken to a new terror: AIDS. The gay community has responded to this tragedy with courage and generosity. The city itself serves as a model for civic intervention and support during a health crisis. The Castro has become less flamboyant and a little more sober in the wake of the crisis; now it's more of a mixed neighborhood, and more relaxed. It is still, however, the center of gay life. Gay bars abound, and gay-oriented boutiques line Castro, 18th, and Market streets.

❽ Across the street from Harvey Milk Plaza is the great neon neighborhood landmark, the **Castro Theatre** marquee. Erected in 1927, the theater is the grandest of San Francisco's few remaining Art Deco movie palaces. Its elaborate Spanish Baroque interior is well preserved, and a new pipe organ plays nightly, ending with a traditional chorus of the Jeanette McDonald standard, "San Francisco." The 1,500-capacity crowd can be enthusiastic and vocal, talking back to the screen as loudly as it talks to them. The Castro Theatre is the showcase for many community events, in particular the annual Gay/ Lesbian Film Festival held each June.

Castro Street boasts numerous men's clothing stores. **All American Boy** (463 Castro St.) is the standard-bearer and setter for casual wear, especially the neighborhood uniform: jeans and T-shirts. Up the street, **Citizen** (536 Castro St.) counters with a more colorful selection of designer-inspired clothing. For athletic wear suitable for sunny days on the street, there's **High Gear** (600 Castro St.).

True to its playful name, **Does Your Mother Know** (4079 18th St.) is a card store like no other, offering specialized greetings to entertain— and shock. Be prepared; this may be the premier X-rated card shop in the country. But some cards are just plain funny, with a stellar series featuring local drag queen Doris Fish, a mistress of many disguises.

A Different Light (489 Castro St.) is not X-rated. It features books by, for, and about lesbians and gay men. The store hosts numerous book-signings and weekly poetry readings.

Time Out The **Patio Cafe** takes advantage of one of the neighborhood's best features: its great weather. You can brunch in an open-air garden court while you get a California tan. The café is inexpensive and serves a standard American fare of omelets, sandwiches, and traditional dinners. Leisurely breakfasts or brunches are the signature meals, accompanied by the weekend-morning drink of choice: mimosas (champagne and orange juice). There's also a full bar. *531 Castro St., tel. 415/621–4640. Open Mon.–Sat. 8 AM–10:30 PM, Sun. 8:45 AM–10:30 PM.*

⑨ Down Market Street **The Names Project** (2363 Market St.) has its offices and public workshop. A gigantic quilt made of more than 10,000 hand-sewn and decorated panels has been pieced together by loved ones to serve as a memorial to those who have died of AIDS. People come from all over the country to work in this storefront as a labor of love and grief; others have sent panels here by mail. New additions to the quilt are always on display. The site serves as a dignified in-process tribute to a community's struggle and compassionate involvement.

Just northwest of Castro and Market streets, an outcropping of rock provides one of the best viewing areas in the city. Walk north up Castro Street two blocks to 16th Street and turn left. This is a steep climb, and it gets steeper and a little more rugged, but it's worth the effort. Turn right at Flint Street; the hill to your left is variously known as Red Rock, Museum Hill, and, correctly, Corona Heights. Start climbing up the path by the tennis courts along the spine of the hill; the view downtown is increasingly superb. You don't have to go very high up to have all of northeast San Francisco and the bay before you. In spring you'll be surrounded by California wildflowers, but whenever you climb to the ragged rocks at the top, be sure to carry a jacket with you: The wind loves this spot.

⑩ At the base of Corona Heights is the **Josephine D. Randall Junior Museum.** Geared toward children by the Recreation and Parks Department, the museum nevertheless has a variety of workshops and events for both young people and their parents. It includes a Mineral Hall, Animal Room, library, and an excellent woodworking studio. *199 Museum Way, tel. 415/554–9600. Open Tues.–Sat. 10–5 and at night for workshops.*

The Castro neighborhood is allied to three events that are true community holidays. In late

> *This trip we found a road less traveled. And the perfect way to see it.*

Vacation Cars. Vacation Prices. Wherever you travel, Budget offers you a wide selection of quality cars – from economy models to roomy minivans and even convertibles. You'll find them all at competitively low rates that include unlimited mileage. At over 1500 locations in the U.S. and Canada. For information and reservations, call your travel consultant or Budget at **800-527-0700**. In Canada, call **800-268-8900**.

THE SMART MONEY IS ON BUDGET.®

We feature Lincoln-Mercury and other fine cars.   *A system of corporate and licensee owned locations.*

No matter what your travel style, the best trips start with **Fodor's**

September or early October, when San Francisco weather is at its warmest, the annual Castro Street Fair takes over several blocks of Castro and Market streets. Huge stages are erected for live music and comedy, alongside booths selling food and baubles. The weather inevitably brings off the men's shirts, and the Castro relives for a moment the permissive spirit of the 1970s.

Each Halloween thousands of revelers (though most are just onlookers) converge on Castro Street from all over the city to watch the perpetual masquerade. Drag queens of all shapes and sizes intentionally reduce the crowd to laughter; the spirit is high and friendly, San Francisco's version of Mardi Gras.

More political is the annual Lesbian/Gay Pride Celebration and Parade, by far the city's largest annual event. On the last Sunday in June 250,000 to 500,000 men and women march to the Civic Center to commemorate the birth of the modern gay-rights movement. This is no longer a parochial march; major political figures participate, and it regularly provides the gay community with its most powerful public statement.

Tour 20: Haight-Ashbury

East of Golden Gate Park is the neighborhood known as "the Haight." Once home to large, middle-class families of European immigrants, the Haight began to change during the late 1950s and early 1960s. Families were fleeing to the suburbs; the big old Victorians were deteriorating or being chopped up into cheap housing. Young people found the neighborhood an affordable and exciting community in which to live according to new precepts.

The peak of the Haight as a youth scene came in 1966. It had become the home of many rock bands. The Grateful Dead moved into a big Victorian at 710 Ashbury Street, just a block off Haight Street. Jefferson Airplane had their grand mansion at 2400 Fulton Street. By 1967, 200,000 young people with flowers in their hair were heading for the Haight. The peace and civil rights movements had made "freedom" their generation's password.

Sharing the late-1980s fascination with things of the 1960s, many visitors to San Francisco want to see the setting of the "Summer of Love." Back in 1967, Gray Lines instituted their "Hippie-Hop," advertising it as "the only foreign tour within the continental limits of the United States," piloted by a driver "especially trained in the sociological significance of the Haight." Today's explorers can walk from Union Square to Market Street and hop aboard Muni's No. 7 Haight.

Haight Street has once again emerged as the center of youth culture in San Francisco, though this time it is an amalgam of punkers, neo-hippies, and suburbanites out to spend their cash. The street has become the city's prime shopping district for "vintage" merchandise. Numerous used-clothing emporiums offer their finery; check out the **New Government** (1427 Haight St.) for '60s and '70s specialties; as well as **Aardvark's**, **Held Over**, and **Buffalo Exchange**, all on the 1500 block. **La Rosa** offers previously worn formal wear for rent and sale (1711 Haight St.). The street also boasts several used-book stores and some of the best used-record stores in the city: **Recycled Records** (1377 Haight St.), **Reckless Records** (1401 Haight St.), and **Rough Trade** (1529 Haight St.) focus on classic rock and roll, obscure independent labels, and hard-to-find imports.

While it increases the incidence of panhandlers and the visibility of the homeless, Golden Gate Park also provides the Haight with unique opportunities for recreation and entertainment. You can rent roller skates at **Skates on Haight** (1818 Haight St.) and roll through the park (it's partially closed to traffic for skaters on Sundays); or you can take the more genteel route and rent bicycles at several stops along Stanyan Street, right by the park's entrance.

The Haight's famous political spirit (it was the first neighborhood in the United States to lead a freeway revolt, and it continues to feature regular boycotts against chain stores said to ruin the street's local character) exists alongside some of the finest Victorian-lined streets in the city;

more than 1,000 such houses occupy the Panhandle and Ashbury Heights streets.

Great city views can be had from **Buena Vista Park** at Haight and Lyon streets. One of San Francisco's most attractive bed-and-breakfast inns is the **Spreckels Mansion** at 737 Buena Vista West, several blocks south of Haight Street. The house was built for sugar baron Richard Spreckels in 1887, and later tenants included Jack London and Ambrose Bierce.

Time Out   Island cuisine—a mix of Cajun, Southwest, and Caribbean influences—is served at **Cha Cha Cha** (1805 Haight St.), which is informal and inexpensive. The decor is technicolor tropical plastic, and the food is hot and spicy. Try the spicy fried calamari or chili-spiked shrimp. *Tel. 415/386–5758. No reservations; expect to wait. No credit cards. Open daily for lunch and dinner.*

What to See and Do with Children

The attractions described in the exploring sections, above, offer a great deal of entertainment for children as well as their families. We suggest, for example, visiting the ships at the **Hyde Street Pier** and spending some time at **Pier 39**, where there is a double-decked Venetian carousel. (*See* Tour 14: The Northern Waterfront, *above.*)

Children will find much to amuse themselves with at **Golden Gate Park**, from the old-fashioned conservatory to the expansive lawns and trails. There is another vintage carousel (1912) at the children's playground. The **Steinhart Aquarium** at the California Academy of Sciences has a "Touching Tide Pool," from which docents will pull starfish and hermit crabs for children or adults to feel. The **Japanese Tea Garden**, although crowded, is well worth exploring; climbing over the high, humpbacked bridges is like moving the neighborhood playground toys into an exotic new (or old) world.

It is also possible to walk across the **Golden Gate Bridge**. The view is thrilling and the wind invigorating, if the children (and adults) are not overwhelmed by the height of the bridge and the nearby automobile traffic. (*See* Tour 15: The Marina and the Presidio, *above*.)

Many children may enjoy walking along crowded Grant Avenue and browsing in the many souvenir shops. Unfortunately, nothing— not even straw finger wrestlers, wooden contraptions to make coins "disappear," shells that open in water to release tissue paper flowers, and other true junk—is as cheap as it once was. (*See* Tour 6: Chinatown, *above*.)

The **San Francisco Zoo**, with a children's zoo, playground, and carousel, is not far from Ocean Beach. The weather and the currents do not allow swimming, but it's a good place for walking and playing in the surf. (*See* Tour 17: Lincoln Park and the Western Shoreline, *above*.)

The **Exploratorium** at the Palace of Fine Arts is a preeminent children's museum and is very highly recommended. (*See* Tour 15: The Marina and the Presidio, *above*.)

Finally, we remind you of the **cable cars**. Try to find time for a ride when the crowds are not too thick (mid-morning or afternoon). It's usually easier to get on at one of the turnarounds at the ends of the lines. (*See* Getting Around by Cable Car in Chapter 1.)

3 Shopping

By Sheila Gadsden

San Franciscan Sheila Gadsden has worked as an editor and writer for such publications as Woman's Day, Motorland, Travel & Leisure, San Francisco, and many others.

San Francisco is a shopper's dream—major department stores, fine fashion, discount outlets, art galleries, and crafts stores are among the many offerings. Most accept at least Visa and MasterCard charge cards, and many also accept American Express, and Diner's Club. A very few accept cash only. Ask about traveler's checks; policies vary. The *San Francisco Chronicle* and *Examiner* advertise sales; for smaller innovative shops, check the San Francisco *Bay Guardian*. Store hours are slightly different everywhere, but a generally trusted rule is to shop between 10 AM and 5 or 6 PM Monday through Saturday (until 8 or 9 PM on Thursday) and from noon until 5 PM on Sunday. Stores on and around Fisherman's Wharf often have longer summer hours.

If you want to cover most of the city, the best shopping route might be to start at Fisherman's Wharf, then continue in order to Union Square and Crocker Galleria, the Embarcadero Center, Jackson Square, Chinatown, North Beach, Chestnut Street, Union Street, Fillmore and Sacramento streets, Japan Center, Haight Street, Civic Center, and South of Market (SoMa).

Major Shopping Districts

Fisherman's Wharf San Francisco's Fisherman's Wharf is host to a number of shopping and sightseeing attractions: **Pier 39, the Anchorage, Ghirardelli Square,** and **The Cannery.** Each offers shops, restaurants, and a festive atmosphere as well as such outdoor entertainment as musicians, mimes, and magicians. Pier 39 includes an amusement area and a double-decked Venetian carousel. One attraction shared by all the centers is the view of the bay and the proximity of the cable car lines, which can take shoppers directly to Union Square.

Union Square San Francisco visitors usually head for shopping at Union Square first. It's centrally located in the downtown area and surrounded by major hotels, from the large luxury properties to smaller bed-and-breakfasts. The square itself is a city park (with a garage underneath). It is flanked by such large stores as **Macy's, Saks Fifth Avenue, I. Magnin,** and **Neiman Marcus. North**

Beach Leather and Gucci are two smaller up-scale stores. Across from the cable car turntable at Powell and Market streets is the San Francisco Shopping Centre, with the fashionable Nordstrom store in the top five floors of shops. Nearby is Crocker Galleria, underneath a glass dome at Post and Kearny streets; 50 shops, restaurants, and services make up this Financial District shopping center, which is topped by two rooftop parks.

Embarcadero Center
Five modern towers of shops, restaurants, and offices plus the Hyatt Regency Hotel make up the downtown Embarcadero Center at the end of Market Street. Like most malls, the center is a little sterile and falls short in the character department. What it lacks in charm, however, it makes up for in sheer quantity. The center's 175 stores and services include such nationally known stores as The Limited, B. Dalton Bookseller, and Ann Taylor, as well as more local or West Coast–based businesses such as the Nature Company, Filian's European Clothing, and Lotus Designer Earrings. Each tower occupies one block, and parking garages are available.

Jackson Square
Jackson Square is where a dozen or so of San Francisco's finest retail antiques dealers are located. If your passion is 19th-century English furniture, for example, there's a good chance that something here will suit. Knowledgeable store owners and staffs can direct you to other places in the city for your special interests. The shops are along Jackson Street in the Financial District, so a visit there will put you very close to the Embarcadero Center and Chinatown.

Chinatown
The intersection of Grant Avenue and Bush Street marks "the Gateway" to Chinatown; here shoppers and tourists are introduced to 24 blocks of shops, restaurants, markets, and temples. There are daily "sales" on gems of all sorts—especially jade and pearls—alongside stalls of bok choy and gingerroot. Chinese silks and toy trinkets are also commonplace in the shops, as are selections of colorful pottery, baskets, and large figures of soapstone, ivory, and jade, including *netsukes* (carved figures).

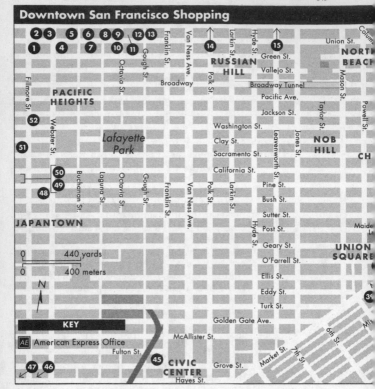

Downtown San Francisco Shopping

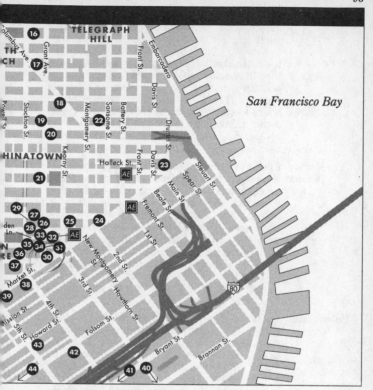

North Beach The once largely Italian enclave of North Beach gets smaller each year as Chinatown spreads northward. It has been called the city's answer to New York City's Greenwich Village, although it's much smaller. Many of the businesses here tend to be small clothing stores, antiques shops, or such eccentric specialty shops as **Quantity Postcard** (1441 Grant Ave., tel. 415/986–8866), which has an inventory of 15,000 different postcards. If you get tired of poking around in the bookstores, a number of cafés dot the streets and there are lots of Italian restaurants.

The Marina District Chestnut Street caters to the shopping needs of Marina District residents. It offers more of a neighborhood feeling than do other well-touristed shopping areas. Banks and well-known stores, including **Waldenbooks, The Gap,** and **Lucca Delicatessen Goods,** are interspersed with such unique gift shops as the **Red Rose Gallerie,** which specializes in "tools for personal growth," including body scents, exotic clothing, and audiotapes for rejuvenating the mind. Shops start at Fillmore Street and end at Broderick Street.

Union Street Out-of-towners sometimes confuse Union Street—a popular stretch of shops and restaurants five blocks south of the Golden Gate National Recreation Area—with downtown's Union Square (*see above*). Nestled at the foot of a hill between the neighborhoods of Pacific Heights and Cow Hollow, Union Street shines with contemporary fashion and custom jewelry. Union Street's feel is largely new and upscale, although there are a few antiques shops and some long-term storekeepers. Shopping here is not limited to wearing apparel, but includes a good bookstore, **Solar Light Books, Union Street Graphics** for posters, and several galleries for crafts, photographs, sculpture, and serigraphs.

Pacific Heights When Pacific Heights residents look for practical services, they look toward Fillmore and Sacramento streets. Both streets feel more like neighborhood streets than upscale shopping areas, and that is exactly their appeal to tourists and natives—easygoing and personal with good bookstores, fine clothing shops, gift shops, thrift stores, and furniture and art galleries.

Sue Fisher King Co. is an eclectic collection of home accessories at 3067 Sacramento Street, and **The Way We Wore** on Fillmore Street offers unusual vintage clothing, including an extensive collection of hats. The Fillmore Street shopping area runs from Post Street to Pacific Avenue. Most shops on the western end of Sacramento Street are between Lyon and Maple streets.

Japantown Unlike Chinatown, North Beach, or the Mission, the 5-acre **Japan Center** (between Geary and Post Sts.) is contained under one roof. It is actually a mall of stores filled with antique kimonos, beautiful tansu chests, and both new and old porcelains. The center always feels a little empty, but the good shops here are well worth a visit. Japan Center occupies the three-block area between Laguna and Fillmore streets, and between Geary and Post streets.

The Haight Haight Street is always an attraction for visitors, if only to see the sign at Haight and Ashbury streets—the geographic center of flower power during the 1960s. These days, instead of tie-dye shirts you'll find good-quality clothing from the 1940s and 1950s, fun jewelry, art from Mexico, and reproductions of Art Deco accessories.

Civic Center The shops and galleries that have sprung up around the Civic Center reflect the cultural offerings of Davies Symphony Hall, Herbst Auditorium, the Opera House, and the Museum of Modern Art. The area is a little sparse compared with other tightly packed shopping streets in the city, but it is well worth a visit. The **San Francisco Opera Shop** at Van Ness Avenue and Grove Street is packed with recordings, books, and posters covering a wide range of music; and the tree-lined block of Hayes Street between Gough and Franklin streets includes art galleries, crafts shops, and pleasant cafés. This area includes Hayes and Grove streets from Polk Street and extends just past Octavia Street.

South of Market South of Market—or SoMa—is where you'll find discount outlets in warehouses next to hip new restaurants and art galleries. At first glance the area doesn't appear to offer very much. But that's only because the streets aren't as spanking-new as some of the more crowded avenues to the north. Venture past the plain doors and down a few alleyways, and you'll see that there's much more than meets the eye.

Department Stores

Emporium (835 Market St., tel. 415/764–2222). This full-service department store carries a complete line of clothing and home furnishings. The prices are reasonable compared with those you'll find at many downtown department stores.

Macy's (Stockton and O'Farrell Sts., tel. 415/397–3333). Designer fashions, an extensive array of shoes, household wares, furniture, food, and even a post office and foreign currency exchange.

Nordstrom (865 Market St., tel. 415/243–8500). Opened in October 1988, this large new downtown store is known for providing excellent service to customers. The building's stunning interior design features spiral escalators circling a four-story atrium. Designer fashions, shoes, accessories, and cosmetics.

Three other large stores that offer high-quality merchandise are **I. Magnin, Neiman Marcus,** and **Saks Fifth Avenue** (all are on Union Square).

Specialty Stores

Antique
Furniture
City of Shanghai (519–521 Grant Ave., tel. 415/982–5520). In business since 1949, this Chinatown store imports unusual collector's items, early dynasty antiques, rare porcelain, Coromandel Coast furniture, silk, jade, and custom-tailored clothing. Hollywood moviemakers rent pieces here to make their sets look more authentic.
Fumiki (2001 Union St., tel. 415/922–0573). This store offers a fine selection of Asian arts, including antiques, art, fine jewelry, Chinese silk paintings, and Korean and Japanese furniture. Two specialties here are *obis* (sashes worn with kimonos) and antique Japanese baskets. Other good sources for Japanese antiques are *Genji* and **Asakichi**, both in Japan Center.
Glen Smith Galleries (2021 Fillmore St., tel. 415/931–3081). The specialties here are 18th- and

19th-century furniture, porcelain, glass, and decorative arts. The gallery is open Tuesday through Saturday from 10 to 5 or by appointment; it is closed noon to 1 PM.

Hunt Antiques (478 Jackson St., tel. 415/989–9531). Fine 17th- to 19th-century period English furniture as well as porcelains, Staffordshire pottery, prints, clocks, and paintings in a gracious country house setting can be found here. This is only one of a dozen or so shops in the Jackson Square area. Others, such as **Foster-Gwin Antiques, Carpets of the Inner Circle,** and the **Antiques Gallery,** are also fine bets.

Telegraph Hill Antiques (580 Union St., tel. 415/982–7055). A very mixed but fine selection is available in this little North Beach shop: fine china and porcelain, crystal, cut glass, Oriental objects, Victoriana, bronzes, and paintings. Open weekdays to 5:30 or by appointment.

Walker McIntyre (3419 Sacramento St., tel. 415/563–8024). This shop specializes in pieces from the Georgian period, but it also offers 19th-century Japanese Imari cloisonné, lamps custom-made from antique vases, and Oriental rugs. Other very fine antiques stores on this street include **Hawley Bragg, Robert Hering,** and **Claire Thomson.**

Antique Jewelry   **J. M. Lang** (323 Sutter St., tel. 415/982–2213). This is another good source for both jewelry and small antique objects, particularly fine glass, amber, and silver.

Old and New Estates (2181-A Union St., tel. 415/346–7525). This shop offers both antique and modern jewelry, crystal, and silver. It is generally open on weekdays and Saturdays from 11 to 6, but the hours do vary, so it's best to call first.

Art Galleries   There are quite a few galleries around the city. The three mentioned here are only a select sample from the Hayes Valley area near the Civic Center.

Images (372 Hayes St., tel. 415/626–2284) specializes in oil paintings and watercolors by northern California realist and impressionist artists. Crafts and jewelry are also on display. Open Tuesday through Saturday.

O'Desso (384 Hayes St., tel. 415/626–5210) is an imaginative collection of paintings, collages, furniture made by artists, crafts, and jewelry. Open Wednesday through Sunday.

Vorpal Gallery (393 Grove St., tel. 415/397–9200). A premier gallery that focuses on postmodern painting, drawing, and sculpture, Vorpal's also has an excellent collection of graphic arts.

Books **City Lights** (261 Columbus Ave., tel. 415/362–8193). The city's most famous bookstore—and possibly the most comfortable bookstore for browsing—this was a major center for poetry readings during the 1960s. City Lights publishes books as well. The store is particularly well stocked in poetry, contemporary literature and music, and translations of third-world literature. There is also an interesting selection of books on nature, the outdoors, and travel. Open daily 10 AM to midnight.

A Clean Well-lighted Place for Books (601 Van Ness Ave., tel. 415/441–6670). You'll find "a large selection of paperbacks and hardbacks in all fields for all ages," particularly books on opera and San Francisco history.

Kinokuniya Bookstores (1581 Webster St., tel. 415/567–7625). This Japan Center store offers all sorts of books and periodicals in Japanese and English, but a major attraction is the collection of beautifully produced graphics and art books. Closed first Tuesday of every month.

Other excellent bookstores in the city include **Solar Light Books** (general needs), **The Sierra Club Bookstore** (California and the West), and **William Stout Architectural Books** (for interiors, exteriors, graphics, and landscape design).

Fabrics **Britex** (146 Geary St., tel. 415/392–2910). This is one of the city's largest collections of fabrics and notions: There are four floors of colors and patterns.

Edward's Unusual Fabrics (80 Geary St., tel. 415/397–5625). This store offers another fine selection of fabrics, especially good silks.

Far East Fashion (953 Grant Ave., tel. 415/362–8171 or 362–0986). Along with **City of Shanghai** (*see above*), this store has one of Chinatown's better selections of Chinese embossed silks and lace.

Fine Gifts and Specialty Items

Biordi (412 Columbus Ave., tel. 415/392–8096). In the heart of North Beach, this small colorful store sells Majolica dinnerware and other imported Italian handicrafts and ceramics.

Gump's (250 Post St., tel. 415/982–1616). Featured at this famous store are jewelry, china, home accessories, stationery, imported goods, and art.

Whittler's Mother (Pier 39, the Embarcadero, tel. 415/433–3010). Handcrafted wood reigns here, including carousel animals—both small and full-size—created and painted on the premises.

Other good specialty stores are **Yone** in North Beach (for beads), the **Sharper Image** downtown (gadgets), and **Waterford Wedgwood** on Union Square (crystal and china).

Clothing for Children

Dottie Doolittle (3680 Sacramento St., tel. 415/563–3244). This store offers domestic and imported clothing sized from infant to 14 years, as well as baby furniture.

Yountville (2453 Fillmore St., tel. 415/922–5050). California and European designs are the draw here, from infant to 8 years.

Clothing for Men and Women

Apacci Paris (50 Grant Ave., tel. 415/982–7222). This exclusive store sells a collection of menswear from Italy, France, and Switzerland. It is known for its unique ties.

Brava Strada (3247 Sacramento St., tel. 415/567–5757). Featured here are designer knitwear, accessories; Italian and other European leather goods; and one-of-a-kind jewelry from American and European artists. Also on Sacramento Street is **Button Down**, carrying "updated traditional" clothing and accessories.

Eileen West (33 Grant Ave., tel. 415/982–2275). San Francisco designer Eileen West displays her lovely dresses, sleepwear, lingerie, linens, and more in this cozy boutique.

Jeanne Marc (262 Sutter St., tel. 415/362–1121). This boutique sells sportswear and more formal clothes in the striking prints that have become the hallmark of this designer.

Justine (3263 Sacramento St., tel. 415/921–8548). Women's clothes by French designers Dorothee Bis, George Rech, and Ventilo are the draw here, as well as shoes by Charles Kammer.

Kilkenny Shop (Ghirardelli Sq., 900 North Point St., tel. 415/771–8984). Irish handwoven shawls, and throws, dresses, tweed hats, and other accessories are sold here.

Krazy Kaps (Pier 39, tel. 415/296–8930). Here you'll find silly hats as well as top hats, Stetsons, and Greek fishermen's caps—a good assortment for personal use and gift giving.

Peluche (3366 Sacramento St., tel. 415/346–6361). This shop specializes in one-of-a-kind, hand-knit sweaters, mostly from Italy, and European fashions for women.

Polo/Ralph Lauren (Crocker Galleria, Post and Kearny Sts., tel. 415/567–7656). This store offers designer apparel and accessories as well as home furnishings.

Sy Aal (1864 Union St., tel. 415/929–1864). Offering "men's fashion with a woman's point of view," Sy Aal carries a full line of fine clothing, including hand-knits, and specializes in ties.

Other good places for women's clothing stores are Union Square; Crocker Galleria, which has such nationally known shops as **Casual Corner**; and the Embarcadero Center, whose selection includes **Ann Taylor, The Limited,** and **Daisy 9 to 5.**

Handicrafts and Folk Art

Cottonwood (3461 Sacramento St., tel. 415/346–6020). Fine handcrafted home furnishings and decorative objects, including flatware, dinnerware, leather boxes, sculpture, and baskets abound in this store.

F. Dorian (388 Hayes St., tel. 415/861–3191). Cards, jewelry, and other crafts from Mexico, Japan, Italy, Peru, Indonesia, Philippines, and Sri Lanka as well as items from local craftspeople are the specialties here.

Folk Art International Gallery (Ghirardelli Sq., 900 North Point St., tel. 415/441–6100). This gallery features an extensive contemporary folk-art collection from Mexico, China, Ecuador, France, Sri Lanka, Peru, Haiti, and other countries—masks, boxes, sculpture, baskets, toys, and textiles. The adjoining gallery, **Xanadu** (tel. 415/441–5211), offers artifacts and tribal art from Asia, Africa, Oceania, and the Americas.

Japonesque (Crocker Galleria, Post and Kearny Sts., tel. 415/ 398–8577). Here you'll find handcrafted wooden boxes, sculpture, paintings, and handmade glass from Japan and the United States.

Ma-Shi'-Ko Folk Craft (1581 Webster St., Japan Center, tel. 415/346–0748). This store carries handcrafted pottery from Japan, including Mashiko, the style that has been in production longer than any other. There are also masks and other handcrafted goods, all from Japan.

Santa Fe (3571 Sacramento St., tel. 415/346–0180). This is where you'll find old Navajo rugs, ranch furniture, old silver and turquoise jewelry, Indian pots and baskets, and cowboy relics.

Smile: A Gallery (1750 Union St., tel. 415/771–1909). A whimsical, colorful collection of folk art, jewelry, and mobiles, including extraordinarily lifelike images of people, created by an artist in Marin.

Virginia Breier (3091 Sacramento St., tel. 415/929–7173). A colorful gallery of contemporary and ethnic crafts from Mexico, Indonesia, Korea, Japan, Brazil, and the United States, especially the West Coast; includes decorative and functional items, antiques.

Yankee Doodle Dandy (1974 Union St., tel. 415/346–0346). A large selection of American antique quilts, carvings, handmade stuffed animals, woven throws.

Other shops to look at are **Oggetti** on Union Street, which carries Italian marbleized papers and gifts, **Designs in Motion** at Pier 39, **Images of the North** on Union Street, **Artifacts** on Fillmore Street, and **Xoxo** on Hayes Street.

Jewelry   **Dai Fook Jewelry** (848 Grant Ave., tel. 415/391–2828). One of many good jewelry stores in Chinatown, this one has good jade, diamonds, and other gems. Two other good jewelry stores in Chinatown are **Empress** and **Jade Empire**, both on Grant Avenue.

Patronik Designs (1949 Union St., tel. 415/922–9716). Innovative contemporary and custom jewelry. Other good stores on Union are **Union Street Goldsmith** and **David Clay**.

Shreve & Co. (Post St. and Grant Ave., tel. 415/421–2600). One of the city's most elegant jewelers, and the oldest retail store in San Francisco, is located near Union Square.

Wholesale Jewelers Exchange (121 O'Farrell St.,

tel. 415/788–2365). This is a source for fine gems and finished jewelry at less than retail prices.

Leather **The Coach Store** (164 Grant Ave., tel. 415/392–1772). A branch of the nationally known purveyor of classically designed leather goods, the inventory here includes purses, briefcases, silk scarves, and belts and wallets of all sizes, colors, and weights.

Malm Luggage (Crocker Galleria at Post and Kearny Sts., tel. 415/391–5222; 222 Grant Ave., tel. 415/392–0417). Fine luggage, leather goods, and accessories.

North Beach Leather (190 Geary St., tel. 415/362–8300). One of the best sources for high-quality leather garments—skirts, jackets, pants, dresses, accessories. With its sculpted walls, the store itself is a work of art. The original store is still in business at Fisherman's Wharf (1365 Columbus Ave., tel. 415/441–3208).

Linens **Claire's Antique Linens & Gifts** (3615 Sacramento St., tel. 415/776–9352). Nationally known for Victorian and Edwardian tablecloths and bedspreads. (The store is true to its name; only about 1% of the items are new.) It also sells crystal and china. Everything is available in a wide range of prices.

Kris Kelly (174 Geary St., tel. 415/986–8822). This lovely store sells imported and domestic handcrafted tablecloths, bed linens, and bath accessories.

Scheuer Linen (318 Stockton St., tel. 415/392–2813). Luxurious linens for the bed, the bath, and the dining table abound here, including European linens and special designs.

Miscellaneous **Aerial** (The Cannery, 2801 Leavenworth St., tel. 415/474–1566). Here you'll find an eclectic mix of goods—soaps, art supplies, handcrafted leather boxes, clothes, pewter flasks, sunglasses, compasses, and lots of unusual but functional objects.

Z Gallerie (2071 Union St., tel. 415/346–9000; Stonestown Galleria, 3251 20th Ave., tel. 415/664–7891). Home furnishings in black—butterfly chairs, dinnerware, desks, chairs, lamps, and a variety of high-tech accessories—are the specialties here; also posters, both black-and-white and color. There are other stores in the San Francisco Shopping Centre on Market Street and on Haight Street.

Sporting Goods **The North Face** (180 Post St. and 1325 Howard St., tel. 415/626–6444). This Bay Area–based company is famous for its top-of-the-line tents, sleeping bags, backpacks, skis, and outdoor apparel, including stylish Gore-tex jackets and pants.

Patagonia (770 Northpoint, near Fisherman's Wharf, tel. 415/771–2050). The outdoorsy set will want to check out Patagonia's signature parkas and jackets at this other famous Bay Area outerwear maker.

Toiletries **The Body Shop** (2072 Union St., tel. 415/922–4076). These are some of the best concoctions around for the face and body—locally produced soaps, lotions, creams, perfumes, and body oils.

Crabtree & Evelyn (50 Post St., Crocker Galleria, Post and Kearny Sts., tel. 415/392–6111; Stonestown Galleria, 19th Ave. and Winston St., tel. 415/753–8015). English and French soaps, shampoos, lotions, creams, shaving supplies, and grooming implements; also jams, assorted condiments, and specialty gifts. Also located at the Embarcadero Center and Ghirardelli Square.

Toys and Gadgets **FAO Schwarz Fifth Avenue** (88 Stockton St., tel. 415/394–8700). The San Francisco branch of an American tradition, this store features a little of everything from games and stuffed toys to motorized cars and trains.

Forma (1715 Haight St., tel. 415/751–0545) is one of the most imaginative shops in the city, with items ranging from design accessories by artists to 1950s-style lava lamps and toy animals inspired by Japanese monster movies.

Kids Only (1415 Haight St., tel. 415/552–5445). A children's emporium, this store has a little bit of everything.

The Sharper Image (532 Market St., tel. 415/398–6472; 680 Davis St. at Broadway, tel. 415/445–6100). This paradise for gadget lovers features everything from five-language translators and super-shock-absorbent tennis racquets to state-of-the-art speaker systems and walkman-size computers. Also at Ghirardelli Square.

Vintage Fashion

Buffalo Exchange (1555 Haight St., tel. 415/431–7733). One of five stores in the Bay Area and in Arizona, the Haight Street store sells both new and recycled clothing and will also trade items. Also at 1800 Polk St.

Held Over (1543 Haight St., tel. 415/684–0818). An extensive collection of clothing from the 1940s, 1950s, and 1960s.

Spellbound (1670 Haight St., tel. 415/863–4930). Fine fashions from decades past—including bugle-beaded dresses, silk scarves, and suits—are offered here. Some of the inventory comes from estate sales.

The Way We Wore (2238 Fillmore St., tel. 415/346–1386). Fashions from the 1920s through the early 1950s are featured here, including an extensive selection of hats.

Vintage Furniture and Accessories

Revival of the Fittest (1701 Haight St., tel. 415/751–8857). Telephones, dishes, assorted collectibles, as well as vintage and reproduction jewelry, clocks, lamps, vases, and furniture can be found here.

The Ritz (1157 Masonic Ave., tel. 415/431–0503). This is a colorful antiques store that offers vintage everything—including jewelry, collectibles, and clocks.

Outlets

A number of clothing factory outlets in San Francisco offer goods at quite reasonable prices. Here are a few of the more popular ones. Outlet maps are available at some of these locations for a nominal fee.

Coat Factory Outlet Store (1350 Folsom St., tel. 415/864–5050). Features discounted coats, jackets, and furs.

Clothing Clearance Center (501 Bryant St., tel. 415/495–7879). You'll find men's casual and business clothing here, as well as women's suits, coats, hats, and shoes.

Esprit (499 Illinois St. at 16 St., south of China Basin, tel. 415/957–2550). Hip sportswear for the young and the young-at-heart at this San Francisco–based company. Savings are 30% to 70% off retail prices.

Loehmann's (222 Sutter St. near Union Square, tel. 415/982-3215.) Many fashionably dressed women swear by Loehman's, where designer labels such as Karl Lagerfeld and Krizia are sold at drastically reduced prices. It helps to know designers, however, as labels are often removed.

My Favorite Clothing and Shoe Store (271 Sutter St., tel. 415/397-8464). Four floors of women's clothes and accessories, including an extensive selection of shoes.

Rainbeau Bodywear Factory Store (300 4th St., tel. 415/777-9786). Excellent-quality exercise gear and dancewear in a wide variety of colors, sizes, and styles.

Six Sixty Center (660 3rd St. at Townsend St., tel. 415/227-0464). There are nearly two dozen outlet stores here, offering apparel, accessories, and shoes for men, women, and children. Open Monday–Saturday.

Yerba Buena Square (899 Howard St. at 5th St., tel. 415/974-5136). The Burlington Coat Factory, with a full range of clothing, is the anchor in this center for apparel, shoes, and toys. It is only two blocks from Market Street, and most of the shops are open daily.

4 Dining

By Jacqueline Killeen

Jacqueline Killeen has been writing about San Francisco restaurants for over 20 years. She is a restaurant critic for San Francisco Focus *magazine.*

San Francisco probably has more restaurants per capita than any city in the United States, including New York. Practically every ethnic cuisine is represented. That makes selecting some seventy restaurants to list here from the vast number available a very difficult task indeed. We have chosen several restaurants to represent each popular style of dining in various price ranges, in most cases because of the superiority of the food, but in some instances because of the view or ambience.

Because we have covered those areas of town most frequented by visitors, this meant leaving out some great places in outlying districts such as Sunset and Richmond. The outlying restaurants we *have* recommended were chosen because they offer a type of experience not available elsewhere.

All listed restaurants serve dinner and are open for lunch unless otherwise specified; restaurants are not open for breakfast unless the morning meal is specifically mentioned.

Parking accommodations are mentioned only when a restaurant has made special arrangements; otherwise you're on your own. There is usually a charge for valet parking. Validated parking is not necessarily free and unlimited; often there is a nominal charge and a restriction on the length of time.

Restaurants do change their policies about hours, credit cards, and the like. It is always best to make inquiries in advance.

The most highly recommended restaurants in each category are indicated by a star ★.

The price ranges listed below are for an average three-course meal. A significant trend among more expensive restaurants is the bar menu, which provides light snacks—hot dogs, chili, pizza, and appetizers—in the bar for a cost that is often less than $10 for two.

Category	Cost*
Very Expensive	over $45
Expensive	$30–$45

Moderate	$18–$30
Inexpensive	under $18

*per person, excluding drinks, service, and 8.5% sales tax

The following credit card abbreviations are used: AE, American Express; DC, Diners Club; MC, MasterCard; V, Visa. Many restaurants accept cards other than those listed here, and some will accept personal checks if you carry a major credit card.

American

Before the 1980s, it was hard to find a decent "American" restaurant in the Bay Area. In recent years, however, the list has been growing and becoming more diversified, with fare that includes barbecue, Southwestern, all-American diner food, and that mix of Mediterranean-Asian-Latino known as California cuisine.

Civic Center **Stars.** This is the culinary temple of Jeremiah
★ Tower, the superchef who claims to have invented California cuisine. Stars is a must stop on every traveling gourmet's itinerary, but it's also where many of the local movers and shakers hang out as well as a popular place for post-theater dining—open till the wee hours. The dining room has a clublike ambience, and the food ranges from grills to ragouts to sautées—some daringly creative and some classical. Dinners here are pricey, but you can eat on a budget with a hot dog at the bar or by standing in line for a table at the informal Star's Cafe next door. *150 Redwood Alley, tel. 415/861-7827. Reservations accepted up to 2 weeks in advance, some tables reserved for walk-ins. Dress: informal. AE, DC, MC, V. No lunch weekends. Closed Thanksgiving, Christmas. Valet parking at night. Expensive.*

Embarcadero **Fog City Diner.** This is where the diner and grazing crazes began in San Francisco, and the popularity of this spot knows no end. The long, narrow dining room emulates a luxurious railroad car with dark wood paneling, huge windows, and comfortable booths. The cooking is innovative, drawing its inspiration from regional cooking throughout the United States. The sharable "small plates" are a fun way to go. *1300 Battery St., tel. 415/982–2000. Reservations advised several weeks in advance for peak hours. Dress: informal. DC, MC, V. Closed Thanksgiving and Christmas. Moderate.*

MacArthur Park. Year after year San Franciscans acclaim this as their favorite spot for ribs, but the oakwood smoker and mesquite grill also turn out a wide variety of all-American fare, from steaks, hamburgers, and chili to seafood. Takeout is also available at this handsomely renovated pre-earthquake warehouse. *607 Front St., tel. 415/398–5700. Reservations advised. Dress: informal. AE, DC, MC, V. No lunch weekends and major holidays. Closed Thanksgiving and Christmas. Valet parking at night. Moderate.*

Financial District **Cypress Club.** Fans of John Cunin have flocked here since 1990 when Masa's long-time maître'd opened his own place, which he calls a "San Francisco brasserie." This categorizes the contemporary American cooking somewhat, but the decor defies description. It could be interpreted as anything from a parody of an ancient temple to a futuristic space war. *500 Jackson St., tel. 415/296–8555. Reservations advised. Dress: informal. AE, DC, MC, V. No lunch Sat. Closed major holidays. Valet parking at night. Expensive.*

Nob Hill **Fournou's Ovens.** There are two lovely dining areas in the elegant Stanford Court Hotel. One is a multilevel room with tiers of tables facing the giant open hearth where many specialties are roasted. Under the direction of chef Lawrence Vito, the restaurant has become known for its imaginative contemporary American cuisine. Many people opt to have breakfast and lunch in the flower-filled greenhouses that flank the hotel and offer views of the cable cars clanking up and down the hill. Wherever you sit, you'll find excellent food and attentive service. *905 California St., tel. 415/989–1910. Reservations advised. Dress: informal. AE, DC, MC, V. Valet parking. Expensive.*

North Beach **Bix.** The owners of Fog City Diner have re-created a '40s supper club in a historic building that was an assay office in Gold Rush days. The place

Downtown San Francisco Dining

Beach St.
North St.
Columbus Ave.
Bay St.
Francisco St.
Chestnut St.
Lombard St.
Embarcadero

Greenwich St.
Filbert St.
Union St.
St.
St.
Way Tunnel
St.
n St.

Taylor St.
Jones St.
Mason St.
Powell St.
Stockton St.
Grant Ave.
Columbus Ave.
Kearny St.
Montgomery St.
Sansome St.
Battery St.
Front St.
Davis St.
Davis St.
Drumm St.
Front St.
Embarcadero
Spear St.
Steuart St.
Main St.
Beale St.
Fremont St.
1st St.
New Montgomery St.
2nd St.
Howard St.
3rd St.
Market St.
Mission St.
5th St.
6th St.
Howard St.
Folsom St.
Harrison St.
Bryant St.
7th St.

KEY

AE American Express Office

0   1/4 mile
0   250 meters

N

Downtown San Francisco Dining

St.

Beach St.

North St.

Columbus Ave.

Bay St.

Francisco St.

Chestnut St.

Lombard St.

Greenwich St.

Filbert St.

Union St.

ay Tunnel

St.

Taylor St.

Mason St.

Jones St.

Powell St.

Stockton St.

Grant Ave.

Kearny St.

Montgomery St.

Sansome St.

Battery St.

Columbus Ave.

Embarcadero

Front St.

Embarcadero

Davis St.

Drumm St.

Front St.

Davis St.

Stewart St.

Spear St.

Main St.

Beale St.

1st St.

Fremont St.

2nd St.

New Montgomery St.

Howard St.

3rd St.

4th St.

5th St.

6th St.

7th St.

Mission St.

Howard St.

Folsom St.

Harrison St.

Bryant St.

Market St.

0   1/4 mile

0   250 meters

KEY

AE American Express Office

N

resembles a theater, with a bustling bar and dining tables downstairs and banquettes on the balcony. Opt for the lower level; the acoustics upstairs are dreadful. The menu offers contemporary renditions of 1940s fare; there's piano music in the evenings. *56 Gold St., tel. 415/433–6300. Reservations advised. Dress: informal. AE, DC, MC, V. No lunch Sat. Valet parking at night. Moderate.*

Washington Square Bar & Grill. You're apt to rub elbows with the city's top columnists and writers in this no-frills saloon. North Beach Italian pasta and seafood dishes mingle with basic bar fare, such as hamburgers and steaks. Pianist at night; open late. *1707 Powell St., tel. 415/982–8123. Reservations advised. Dress: informal. AE, DC, MC, V. Closed most major holidays. Validated parking at garage around the corner on Filbert St. Moderate.*

Pacific Heights

Perry's. The West Coast equivalent of P.J. Clarke's in Manhattan, this popular watering hole and meeting place for the button-down singles set serves good, honest saloon food—London broil, corned beef hash, one of the best hamburgers in town, and a great breakfast. Breakfast is served on weekends. *1944 Union St., tel. 415/922–9022. Reservations accepted. Dress: informal. AE, MC, V. Closed Thanksgiving, Christmas. Moderate.*

South of Market

Asta. Named after Nick and Nora's dog in "The Thin Man" series, this new spot is a time capsule of the '30s, with flicks of the famous sleuths on VCRs in the bar. The food, however, is in tune with the 1990s, with bright, creative versions of all-time American favorites and down-home desserts. Dancing Friday and Saturday nights. *Rincon Center, 101 Spear St., 415/495–2782. Reservations accepted. Dress: informal. AE, MC, V. No lunch Sat., no dinner Mon., closed Sun. Validated parking at Rincon Center garage. Moderate.*

Harry Denton's. Every night's a party at this new waterfront hangout, where singles congregate in a Barbary Coast–style bar and the rugs are rolled up at 10 o'clock for dancing in the dining room. Sometimes Harry himself–the city's best-known saloon keeper–even dances on the bar. But at lunchtime the place is quieter, at-

tracting diners with its f
saloon food: cheesy oni
loaf, pot roast, *cioppi*
like. *161 Steuart St.*
vations advised. Dr
V. Closed Thanks,
Year's Day. Valet parking
Moderate.

Union Square **Campton Place.** This elegant, ultrasop
★ cated small hotel put new American cooking on
the local culinary map. Although opening chef,
Bradley Ogden, is now at his own place (the
Lark Creek Inn in Marin County), his successor
at Campton Place, Jan Birnbaum, carries on
Ogden's innovative traditions with great
aplomb and has added his own touches from
breakfast and Sunday brunch (one of the best in
town) through the dinner hours. A bar menu offers some samplings of appetizers, plus a caviar
extravaganza. *340 Stockton St., tel. 415/781-*
5155. Reservations suggested, 2 weeks in ad-
vance on weekends. Jacket required at dinner,
tie requested. AE, DC, MC, V. Valet parking.
Expensive.

★ **Postrio.** This is the place for those who want to
see and be seen: There's always a chance to
catch a glimpse of some celebrity, including
Postrio's owner, superchef Wolfgang Puck, who
periodically commutes from Los Angeles to
make an appearance in the restaurant's open
kitchen. A stunning three-level bar and dining
area is highlighted by palm trees and museum-
quality contemporary paintings. The food is
Puckish Californian with Mediterranean and
Asian overtones, emphasizing pastas, grilled
seafood, and house-baked breads. A substantial
breakfast and bar menu are served here, too.
545 Post St., tel. 415/776-7825. Reservations
advised. Jacket and tie suggested. AE, DC, MC,
V. Valet parking. Expensive–Very Expensive.

Chinese

For nearly a century, Chinese restaurants in
San Francisco were confined to Chinatown and
the cooking was largely an Americanized version of peasant-style Cantonese. The past few
decades, however, have seen an influx of restaurants representing the wide spectrum of Chi-

nese cuisine: the subtly seasoned fare of Canton, the hot and spicy cooking of Hunan and Szechuan, the northern style of Peking, where meat and dumplings replace seafood and rice as staples, and, more recently, some more esoteric cooking, such as Hakka and Chao Chow. The current rage seems to be the high-style influence of Hong Kong. These restaurants are now scattered throughout the city, leaving Chinatown for the most part to the tourists.

Embarcadero ★ **Harbor Village.** Classic Cantonese cooking, dim sum lunches, and fresh seafood from the restaurant's own tanks are the hallmarks of this 400-seat branch of a Hong Kong establishment, which sent five of its master chefs to San Francisco to supervise the kitchen. The setting is opulent, with Chinese antiques and teak furnishings. *4 Embarcadero Center, tel. 415/781–8833. Reservations not accepted for lunch on weekends. Dress: informal. AE, DC, MC, V. Free validated parking in Embarcadero Center Garage. Moderate.*

Financial District **Yank Sing.** This teahouse has grown by leaps and branches with the popularity of dim sum. The Battery Street location seats 300 and the older, smaller Stevenson Street site has recently been rebuilt in high-tech style. *427 Battery St., tel. 415/362–1640. 49 Stevenson St., tel. 415/495–4510. Reservations advised. Dress: informal. AE, MC, V. No dinner. Stevenson site closed weekends. Inexpensive.*

North Beach **Fortune.** The Chao Chow tradition of the southern coast of China is well represented in this small restaurant on the edge of Chinatown. Among the complexly seasoned dishes for which Chao Chow cooking is most noted are braised duck with a garlicky vinegar sauce and an eggy oyster cake. *675 Broadway, tel. 415/421–8130. Dress: informal. MC, V. Inexpensive.*

Hunan. Henry Chung's first café on Kearny Street had only six tables, but his Hunanese cooking merited six stars from critics nationwide. He has now opened this larger place on Sansome Street; it's equally plain but has 250 seats. Smoked dishes are a specialty, and Henry guarantees no MSG. *924 Sansome St., tel. 415/*

You've Let Your Imagination Go, Now Get Up And Follow Your Dreams.

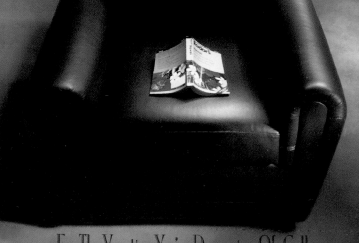

For The Vacation You're Dreaming Of, Call American Express Travel Agency At 1-800-YES-AMEX.

American Express will send more than your imagination soaring. We'll fly you, sail you, drive you to any Fodor's destination and beyond. Because American Express believes the best vacations happen from Europe to the Orient, Walt Disney World to Hawaii and everywhere in between.

For dependable service, expert advice, and value wherever your dreams take you, call on American Express. After all, the best traveling companion is a trustworthy friend.

It's easy to recognize a good place when you see one.

American Express Cardmembers have been doing it for years.

The secret? Instead of just relying on what they see in the window, they look at the door. If there's an American Express Blue Box on it, they know they've found an establishment that cares about high standards.

Whether it's a place to eat, to sleep, to shop, or simply meet, they know they will be warmly welcomed.

So much so, they're rarely taken in by anything else.

Always a good sign.

956–7727. Reservations advised. Dress: informal. AE, DC, MC, V. Inexpensive.

Northern Waterfront

The Mandarin. Owner Cecilia Chiang introduced San Franciscans to the full spectrum of Chinese cooking in 1961 in a tiny Post Street locale, then moved to this magnificent setting, decorated with paintings and embroideries from her family's palatial homes in Peking. Though Madam Chiang has retired, the new owners have expanded upon her traditions with the addition of a dim sum lunch. The finest offerings, such as Mandarin duck, beggar's chicken cooked in clay, and the Mongolian fire pot, must be ordered a day in advance. Bay view from some tables. *Ghirardelli Sq., tel. 415/673–8812. Reservations advised. Dress: informal. AE, DC, MC, V. Closed Thanksgiving, Christmas. Validated parking in Ghirardelli Sq. garage. Moderate–Expensive.*

Richmond
★

Hong Kong Flower Lounge. Many Chinaphiles swear that this outpost of a famous Asian restaurant chain serves the best Cantonese food in town. The seafood is spectacular, as is the dim sum. *5322 Geary Blvd., tel. 415/668–8998. Reservations advised. Dress: informal. AE, MC, V. Moderate.*

South of Market

Wu Kong. Tucked away in the splashy Art Deco Rincon Center, Wu Kong features the cuisine of Shanghai and Canton. Specialties include dim sum; braised yellow fish; and the incredible vegetable goose, one of the Asian city's famous mock dishes, created from paper-thin layers of dried bean-curd sheets and mushrooms. *101 Spear St., tel. 415/957–9300. Reservations advised. Dress: informal. AE, DC, MC, V. Validated parking at Rincon Center garage. Moderate.*

French

French cooking has gone in and out of vogue in San Francisco since the extravagant days of the Bonanza Kings. A renaissance of the classic haute cuisine occurred during the 1960s, but recently a number of these restaurants closed. Meanwhile, nouvelle cuisine went in and out of fashion, and the big draw now is the bistro or brasserie.

Civic Center   **California Culinary Academy.** This historic theater houses one of the most highly regarded professional cooking schools in the United States.
Watch the student chefs at work on the double-
tiered stage while you dine on classic French
cooking. Prix-fixe meals and bountiful buffets
are served in the main dining room; heart-
healthy à la carte lunches are served at Cyril's
on the balcony level, and there's a grill on the
first floor. *625 Polk St., tel. 415/771–3500. Reservations advised (2–4 weeks for Fri.-night buffet). Jacket and tie requested, but not required.
AE, DC, MC, V. Closed weekends and major
holidays. Moderate–Expensive.*

Financial   **Le Central.** This is the quintessential bistro:
District   noisy and crowded, with nothing subtle about
the cooking. But the garlicky pâtés, leeks vinai-
grette, cassoulet, and grilled blood sausage
with crisp french fries keep the crowds coming.
*453 Bush St., tel. 415/ 391–2233. Reservations
advised. Dress: informal. AE, MC, V. Closed
Sun. and major holidays. Moderate.*

Marina   **Rodin.** The nouvelle cuisine is as artful as the
Rodin sculptures that decorate this little jewel
of a neighborhood restaurant. And the service is
ever-so-caring. Dinners are both prix fixe and à
la carte. *1779 Lombard St., tel. 415/563–8566.
Reservations advised. Dress: informal. DC,
MC, V. No lunch. Closed Sun. and major holidays. Nominal charge for parking in motel next
door. Expensive.*

Midtown   **La Folie.** This pretty storefront café showcases
the nouvelle cuisine of Roland Passot, a former
sous chef at Illinois' famous Le Français. Much
of the food is edible art—whimsical presenta-
tions that recall palm trees or peacocks; even
a soup garnish that looks like a giant ladybug.
The fun spirit of the place lets you forgive the
sometimes lackadaisical, though well-inten-
tioned, service. *2316 Polk St., tel. 415/776–
5577. Reservations advised. Dress: informal.
AE, DC, MC, V. No lunch. Closed Sun. Expensive.*

North Beach   **Ernie's.** This famous old-timer recently had a
★   face-lift, and Alain Rondelli, one of France's
most promising young chefs, is now in charge of
the kitchen, preparing innovative light versions

of French classics. Even so, Ernie's is still steeped with the aura of Gay Nineties San Francisco and is about the only place in town that offers tableside service. You will pay dearly for dinner, but the prix fixe, three-course lunch is a bargain. *847 Montgomery St., tel. 415/397-5969. Reservations advised. Jacket and tie required. AE, DC, MC, V. No lunch Sat.–Mon. Closed major holidays. Valet parking. Very Expensive.*

South of Market ★ **Fringale.** The fresh yellow paint of this dazzling new bistro stands out like a beacon on an otherwise bleak industrial street, attracting a Pacific Heights-Montgomery Street clientele. They come for the food–the French Basque–inspired creations of Biarritz-born chef Gerald Hirigoyen–at remarkably reasonable prices. Hallmarks include Roquefort ravioli, rare ahi (a rare kind of tuna) with onion marmalade, and the ultimate crème brulée. *570 Fourth St., tel. 415/543-0573. Reservations required. Dress: informal. MC, V. No lunch Sat. Closed Sun., Thanksgiving, Christmas, and New Year's Day. Moderate.*

Union Square ★ **Masa's.** Chef Julian Serrano carries on the tradition of the late Masa Kobayashi. In fact, some Masa regulars even say the cooking is better. The artistry of the presentation is as important as the food itself in this pretty, flower-filled dining spot in the Vintage Court Hotel. *648 Bush St., tel. 415/989-7154. Reservations should be made precisely 21 days in advance. Jacket required. AE, DC, MC, V. No lunch. Closed Sun., Mon., 1st week in July, last week in Dec., 1st week in Jan. Valet parking. Very Expensive.*

★ **Fleur de Lys.** The creative cooking of chef/partner Hubert Keller is drawing rave reviews to this romantic spot that some now consider the best French restaurant in town. The menu changes constantly, but such dishes as lobster soup with lemongrass are a signature. The intimate dining room, like a sheikh's tent, is encased with hundreds of yards of paisley. *777 Sutter St., tel. 415/673-7779. Reservations on weekends advised 2 weeks in advance. Jacket required. AE, DC, MC, V. No lunch. Closed Sun., Thanksgiving, Christmas, New Year's Day. Valet parking. Very Expensive.*

Greek and Middle Eastern

The foods of Greece and the Middle East have much in common: a preponderance of lamb and eggplant dishes, a widespread use of phyllo pastry, and an abundance of pilaf.

North Beach **Maykadeh.** Here you'll find authentic Persian cooking in a setting so elegant that the modest check comes as a great surprise. Lamb dishes with rice are the specialties. *470 Green St., tel. 415/362–8286. Reservations advised. Dress: informal. MC, V. Valet parking at night. Inexpensive–Moderate.*

South of **S. Asimakopoulos Cafe.** Terrific Greek food at
Market reasonable prices keeps the crowds waiting for seats at the counter or at bare-topped tables in this storefront café. The menu is large and varied, but lamb dishes are the stars. Convenient to Showplace Square. *288 Connecticut, Potrero Hill, tel. 415/552–8789. No reservations. Dress: informal. AE, MC, V. No lunch weekends. Closed major holidays. Inexpensive–Moderate.*

Indian

The following restaurants serve the cuisine of northern India, which is more subtly seasoned and not as hot as its southern counterparts. They also specialize in succulent meats and crispy breads from the clay-lined tandoori oven.

Northern **Gaylord's.** A vast selection of mildly spiced
Waterfront northern Indian food is offered here, along with
and meats and breads from the tandoori ovens and a
Embarcadero wide range of vegetarian dishes. The dining rooms are elegantly appointed with Indian paintings and gleaming silver service. The Ghirardelli Square location offers bay views. *Ghirardelli Sq., tel. 415/771–8822. Embarcadero One, tel. 415/397–7775. Reservations advised. Dress: informal. AE, DC, MC, V. No lunch Sun. at Embarcadero. Closed Thanksgiving, Christmas. Validated parking at Ghirardelli Sq. garage and Embarcadero Center garage. Moderate.*

Pacific **North India.** Small and cozy, this restaurant has
Heights a more limited menu and hotter seasoning than Gaylord. Both tandoori dishes and curries are served, plus a range of breads and appetizers.

Everything is cooked to order. *3131 Webster St.,
tel. 415/931–1556. Reservations advised. Dress:
informal. AE, DC, MC, V. No lunch weekends.
Parking behind restaurant. Moderate.*

Italian

Italian food in San Francisco spans the "boot"
from the mild cooking of northern Italy to the
spicy cuisine of the south. Then there is the style
indigenous to San Francisco, known as North
Beach Italian—such dishes as *cioppino* (a
fisherman's stew) and Joe's special (a mélange of
eggs, spinach, and ground beef).

Embarcadero **Il Fornaio.** An offshoot of the Il Fornaio bakeries, this handsome tile-floored, wood-paneled
complex combines a café, bakery, and upscale
trattoria with outdoor seating. The cooking is
Tuscan, featuring pizzas from a wood-burning
oven, superb house-made pastas and gnocchi,
and grilled poultry and seafood. Anticipate a
wait for a table, but once seated, you won't be
disappointed—only surprised by the moderate
prices. *Levi's Plaza, 1265 Battery, tel. 415/986–
0100. Reservations advised. Dress: informal.
AE, MC, V. Closed Thanksgiving, Christmas.
Valet parking. Moderate.*

Financial **Blue Fox.** This landmark restaurant was revita-
District lized in 1988 by Gianni Fassio, son of a former
owner, who redecorated the place in a low-key,
formal style. The classic cooking is from northern Italy, with a seasonally changing menu.
Pasta and gnocchi are made on the premises, as
are the luscious desserts. *659 Merchant St., tel.
415/981–1177. Reservations required. Jacket
and tie required. AE, DC, MC, V. Dinner only.
Closed Sun. and major holidays. Valet parking.
Expensive–Very Expensive.*

Marina **Ristorante Parma.** This is a warm, wonderfully
honest trattoria with excellent food at modest
prices. The antipasti tray, with a dozen unusual
items, is one of the best in town, and the pastas
and veal are exceptional. Don't pass up the spinach gnocchi when it is offered. *3314 Steiner St.,
tel. 415/567–0500. Reservations advised. Dress:
informal. AE, MC, V. No lunch. Closed Sun.
and some major holidays. Moderate.*

Midtown **Acquarello.** This exquisite restaurant is a ven-
★ ture of the former chef and former maître 'd at
Donatello. The service and food are exemplary,
and the menu covers the full range of Italian cuisine, from northern Italy to the tip of the boot.
Desserts are exceptional. *1722 Sacramento St.,
tel. 415/567–5432. Reservations advised. Dress:
informal. DC, MC, V. No lunch. Closed Sun.–
Mon. Validated parking across the street.
Moderate–Expensive.*

Tutto Bene. Despite its dazzling decor, this upscale trattoria was off to a slow start until culinary wizard Tony Gulisano took over the kitchen
in 1991. Now the pastas and polentas, grilled
meats, and seafoods on the ever-changing menu
have critics and the cognoscenti raving. Live
music at night. *2080 Van Ness Ave., tel. 415/
673–3500. Reservations advised. Dress: informal. AE, DC, MC, V. No lunch. Closed Sun.,
Mon. Valet parking. Moderate.*

North Beach **Buca Giovanni.** Giovanni Leoni showcases the
★ dishes of his birthplace: the Serchio Valley in
Tuscany. Pastas made on the premises are a specialty, and the calamari salad is one of the best
around. The subterranean dining room is cozy
and romantic. *800 Greenwich St., tel. 415/776–
7766. Reservations advised. Dress: informal.
AE, DC, MC, V. No lunch. Closed Sun. and
most major holidays. Moderate.*

Capp's Corner. One of the last of the family-style
trattorias, diners sit elbow to elbow at long For-
mica tables to feast on bountiful five-course
dinners. For the budget-minded or calorie-
counters, a shorter dinner includes a tureen of
soup, salad, and pasta. *1600 Powell St., North
Beach, tel. 415/989–2589. Reservations advised. Dress: informal. DC, MC, V. No lunch
weekends. Closed Thanksgiving, Christmas.
Credit off meal check for parking in garage
across the street. Inexpensive.*

Teatro. The unpretentious exterior of this new
ristorante belies the refinement of food and
service within. Owners Francesco Giacomarra
and Patrizio Sacchetto pay the same attention
to quality and detail as they did at the venerable
Blue Fox, where they served as maître d' and
chef. The northern Italian cooking bears the im-
print of Piedmont, Sacchetto's birthplace. *641*

Vallejo, tel. 415/399-0855. Reservations advised. Dress: informal. No lunch. Closed Sun. and Mon. Moderate-Expensive.

South of Market

★

Etrusca. The ancient Etruscan civilization inspired this popular showplace in Rincon Center. Onyx chandeliers cast a warm glow on Siena gold walls, terrazzo floors, and ceiling frescoes. The dishes from the giant wood-fire oven that dominates the open kitchen, however, recall modern Tuscany more than ancient Etruria. Bar menu. *Rincon Center, 101 Spear St., tel. 415/777-0330. Reservations advised. Dress: informal. AE, MC, V. No lunch weekends. Validated parking in Rincon Center garage, valet service at night. Moderate.*

Undici. The robust flavors of Sicily and Sardinia dominate the menu of this SoMa hot spot. Along with pastas and pizzas, look for earthy soups and stews. *374 11th St., tel. 415/431-3337. Reservations advised. Dress: informal. DC, MC, V. No lunch Sat. Closed Sun. Moderate.*

Union Square

Vinoteca Jackson Fillmore. Though new to the restaurant scene in 1991, chef Jack Krietzman's unpretentious café trattoria looks like an old-timer from North Beach or even Italy itself, with bentwood chairs, checkered cloths, and wooden floors. Krietzman calls it "a normal place for normal people serving normal food." The food is way beyond the norm, however, boasting lots of garlic, anchovies, and the robust flavors of southern Italy. They also serve one of the frothiest zabagliones in town. There is a bar menu. *586 Bush St., tel. 415/983-6200. Dress: informal. AE, DC, MC, V. No lunch weekends. Moderate.*

Japanese

To understand a Japanese menu, you should be familiar with the basic types of cooking: *yaki,* marinated and grilled foods; *tempura,* fish and vegetables deep-fried in a light batter; *udon* and *soba,* noodle dishes; *domburi,* meats and vegetables served over rice; *ramen,* noodles served in broth; and *nabemono,* meals cooked in one pot, often at the table. Of course sushi bars are extremely popular in San Francisco; most offer a selection of *sushi,* vinegared rice with fish or vegetables, and *sashimi*, raw fish. Western seating refers to conventional tables and chairs; *tatami* seating is on mats at low tables.

Chinatown **Yamato.** The city's oldest Japanese restaurant is by far its most beautiful, with inlaid wood, painted panels, a meditation garden, and a pool. Both Western and tatami seating, in private shoji-screened rooms, are offered, along with a fine sushi bar. Come primarily for the atmosphere; the menu is somewhat limited, and more adventurous dining can be found elsewhere. *717 California St., tel. 415/397–3456. Reservations advised. AE, DC, MC, V. No lunch weekends. Closed Mon., Thanksgiving, Christmas, New Year's Day. Moderate.*

Japantown **Sanppo.** This small place has an enormous selection of almost every type of Japanese food: yakis, nabemono dishes, domburi, udon, and soba, not to mention feather-light tempura and interesting side dishes. Western seating only. *1702 Post St., tel. 415/346–3486. No reservations. Dress: informal. No credit cards. Closed Mon. and major holidays. Validated parking in Japan Center garage. Inexpensive.*

Mediterranean

In its climate and topography, its agriculture and viticulture, and the orientation of many of its early settlers, northern California resembles the Mediterranean region. But until quite recently no restaurant billed itself as "Mediterranean." Those that do so now primarily offer a mix of southern French and northern Italian food, but some include accents from Spain, Greece, and more distant ports of call.

Civic Center **Zuni Cafe Grill.** Zuni's Italian-Mediterranean
★ menu and its unpretentious atmosphere pack in the crowds from early morning to late evening. A balcony dining area overlooks the large bar, where both shellfish and drinks are dispensed. A second dining room houses the giant pizza oven and grill. Even the hamburgers have an Italian accent: They're served on herbed focaccia buns. *1658 Market St., tel. 415/552–2522. Dress: informal. Reservations advised. AE, MC, V. Closed Mon., Thanksgiving, Christmas. Moderate–Expensive.*

Embarcadero **Splendido's.** Mediterranean cooking is the focus at this handsome new restaurant. Diners here are transported to the coast of southern France or northern Italy by the pleasant decor. Among the many winners are the shellfish soup, warm goat cheese and ratatouille salad, *pissaladiere* (the pizza of Provence), and pan-roasted quail with white truffle pasta. Desserts are truly *splendido*. Bar menu. *Embarcadero Four, tel 415/986–3222. Reservations advised. Dress: informal. AE, DC, MC, V. No lunch weekends. Validated parking at Embarcadero Center garage. Moderate.*

★ **Square One.** Chef Joyce Goldstein introduces an ambitious new menu daily, with dishes based on the classic cooking of the Mediterranean countries, although she sometimes strays to Asia and Latin America. The dining room, with its views of the open kitchen and the Golden Gateway commons, is an understated setting for some of the finest food in town. Bar menu. *190 Pacific Ave., tel. 415/788–1110. Reservations advised. Dress: informal. AE, DC, MC, V. No lunch weekends. Closed major holidays. Valet parking in evenings. Moderate–Expensive.*

Union Square **Lascaux.** Despite its Gallic name (after the painted caves in France), the cuisine at this smart new restaurant is primarily Mediterranean, with a contemporary Italian accent. Of particular note are the appetizers (such as sun-dried tomato and mascarpone torta, or the various takes on polenta), split-roasted meats, and grilled seafood with zesty sauces. A huge fireplace cheers the romantically lighted subterranean dining room. Live jazz at night. *248 Sutter St., tel. 415/391–1555. Reservations advised. Dress: informal. AE, DC, MC, V. No lunch Sat. Closed Sun., Thanksgiving, Christmas. Moderate.*

Mexican/Latin American

In spite of San Francisco's Mexican heritage, until recently most south-of-the-border eateries were locked into the Cal-Mex taco-enchilada-mashed-beans syndrome. But now some newer places offer a broader spectrum of Mexican and Latin American cooking.

South of **Chevys.** This first San Francisco branch of a pop-
Market ular Mexican minichain is decked out with funky
neon signs and "El Machino" turning out flour
tortillas. "Stop gringo food" is the motto here,
and the emphasis is on the freshest ingredients
and sauces. Of note are the fabulous fajitas and
the grilled quail and seafood. *4th and Howard
Sts., tel. 415/543–8060. Reservations accepted
only for parties of 8 or more. Dress: informal.
MC, V. Closed Christmas. Validated parking
evenings and weekends at garage under bldg.
(enter from Minna St.). Inexpensive.*

Union Square **Corona Bar & Grill.** The ever-changing menu of-
★ fers light versions of regional Mexican dishes.
Corona's paella, laden with shellfish and
calamari, is sensational, as is the chocolate-
coated flan. The atmosphere is a mix of old San
Francisco (pressed tin ceilings and an antique
bar) and old Mexico (hand-painted masks and
Aztec motifs). *88 Cyril Magnin St., tel. 415/
392–5500. Reservations advised. Dress: informal. AE, DC, MC, V. Closed Thanksgiving,
Christmas. Moderate.*

Old San Francisco

Several of the city's landmark restaurants just
don't fit neatly into any ethnic category. Some
might call them Continental or French or even
American. But dating back to the turn of the
century or earlier, these places all exude the
traditions and aura of old San Francisco. The
oldest one of them all, Tadich Grill, is listed under Seafood.

Financial **Garden Court, Palace Hotel.** After a massive,
District two-year, multimillion-dollar renovation, the
Garden Court of the Sheraton Palace has re-
emerged as the ultimate old San Francisco éxpe-
rience. From breakfast through lunch, teatime,
and the early dinner hours, light splashes
through the $7 million stained-glass ceiling
against the towering Ionic columns and crystal
chandeliers. The classic European menu highlights many famous dishes devised by Palace
chefs during the early years of this century, and
the extravagant Sunday buffet brunch again
takes center stage as one of the city's great traditions. *Market and New Montgomery Sts., tel.*

415/546–5000. *Reservations advis*
and tie required at dinner. AE, DC, M ,
pensive.

Jack's. Little has changed in more than 1〇〇
years at this bankers' and brokers' favorite. The
menu is extensive, but regulars opt for the simple fare—steaks, chops, seafood, and stews.
The dining room has an old-fashioned, no-non-
sense aura, and private upstairs rooms are
available for top-secret meetings. *615 Sacra-*
mento St., tel. 415/986–9854. Reservations ad-
vised. Jacket required. AE. No lunch weekends.
Closed major holidays. Moderate.

Union Square **Bardelli's.** Founded in 1906 as Charles' Oyster
House, this turn-of-the-century showplace
boasts high-vaulted ceilings, massive marble
columns, and stained glass. The menu mixes
French, Italian, and American fare with superb
fresh seafood. *243 O'Farrell St., tel. 415/982–*
0243. Reservations accepted. Dress: informal.
AE, DC, MC, V. No lunch Sat. Closed Sun. Val-
idated parking at Downtown Center garage.
Moderate.

Seafood

Like all port cities, San Francisco takes pride in
its seafood, even though less than half the fish
served here is from local waters. In winter and
spring look for the fresh Dungeness crab, best
served cracked with mayonnaise. In summer,
feast upon Pacific salmon, even though imported
varieties are available year-round. A recent development is the abundance of unusual oysters
from West Coast beds and an outburst of oyster
bars.

Civic Center **Hayes Street Grill.** Eight to 15 different kinds of
★   seafood are chalked on the blackboard each
night at this extremely popular restaurant. The
fish is served simply grilled, with a choice of
sauces ranging from tartar to a spicy Szechuan
peanut concoction. Appetizers are unusual, and
desserts are lavish. *320 Hayes St., tel. 415/863–*
5545. Reservations should be made precisely 1
week in advance. Dress: informal. AE, MC, V.
No lunch Sat. Closed Sun. and major holidays.
Moderate.

Grill. Sam's and Tadich (below) are two of ~~ci~~ty's oldest restaurants and so popular for ~~lunc~~h that you must arrive before 11:30 to get ~~a t~~able. No frills here. The aura is starkly ~~old~~-fashioned; some booths are enclosed and ~~cu~~rtained. Although the menu is extensive and ~~v~~aried, those in the know stick with the fresh local seafood and East Coast shellfish. *374 Bush St., tel. 415/421–0594. Reservations accepted only for parties of 6 or more. Dress: informal. AE, DC, MC, V. Closed weekends and holidays. Moderate.*

Tadich Grill. Owners and locations have changed many times since this old-timer opened during the Gold Rush era, but the 19th-century atmosphere remains, as does the kitchen's special way with seafood. Seating at the counter or in private booths; long lines for a table at lunchtime. *240 California St., tel. 415/391–2373. No reservations. Dress: informal. MC, V. Closed Sun. and holidays. Moderate.*

Northern Waterfront

McCormick & Kuleto's. This new seafood emporium in Ghirardelli Square is a visitor's dream come true: a fabulous view of the bay from every seat in the house; an old San Francisco atmosphere; and some 30 varieties of fish and shellfish prepared in some 70 globe-circling ways, from tacos, pot stickers, and fish cakes to grills, pastas, and stew. The food does have its ups and downs, however, but even on foggy days you can count on the view. *Ghirardelli Square, tel. 415/929–1730. Reservations advised. Dress: informal. AE, DC, MC, V. Closed major holidays. Validated parking in Ghirardelli Square garage. Moderate.*

Pacific Heights

Pacific Heights Bar & Grill. This is unquestionably the best oyster bar in town, with at least a dozen varieties available each day and knowledgeable shuckers to explain the mollusks' origins. In the small dining rooms, grilled seafood and shellfish stews head the bill of fare. Paella is a house specialty. *2001 Fillmore St., tel. 415/567–3337. Reservations advised. Dress: informal. AE, DC, MC, V. No lunch. Closed Thanksgiving, Christmas. Moderate.*

Union Square

Bentley's Oyster Bar & Restaurant. The bustling bar downstairs dispenses at least 10 different types of oysters. An upstairs dining room offers the eclectic seafood concoctions of chef Amey Shaw, who mixes and matches the hot-and-spicy flavors of Southeast Asia, the American Southwest, and the Mediterranean. *185 Sutter St., tel. 415/989–6895. Reservations advised. Dress: informal. AE, DC, MC, V. Closed major holidays. Validated parking at downstairs garage in the evening. Moderate.*

Southeast Asian

In recent years San Franciscans have seen tremendous growth in the numbers of restaurants specializing in the foods of Thailand, Vietnam, and, most recently, Cambodia. The cuisines of these countries share many features, and one characteristic in particular: The cooking is always spicy and often very hot.

Civic Center
★ **Monsoon.** This brilliant new restaurant combines the cuisines of China and Southeast Asia, most notably Thailand. The concept of a pan-Asian menu is common in many of China's coastal cities, and was adapted here by Monsoon founder Bruce Cost, one of the foremost authorities on Asian food in the United States. The subtle surroundings are highlighted by contemporary Asian ceramics. *Opera Plaza, 601 Van Ness Ave., tel. 415/441–3232. Reservations advised. Dress: informal. MC, V. Closed Mon. Moderate.*

Marina **Angkor Palace.** This is one of the loveliest Cambodian restaurants in town and also the most conveniently located for visitors. The extensive family-style menu offers such exotic fare as fish-and-coconut mousse baked in banana leaves. You'll have questions, of course, but you'll find the staff eager to explain the contents of the menu. *1769 Lombard St., tel. 415/931–2830. Reservations advised. Dress: informal. AE, MC, V. No lunch. Inexpensive.*

Richmond District
★ **Khan Toke Thai House.** The city's first Thai restaurant has a lovely dining room, furnished with low tables and cushions, and a garden view. The six-course dinners, with two entrées from an extensive choice, provide a delicious introduction to Thai cooking. (The seasoning will be mild, unless you request it hot.) Classical Thai dancing

on Sunday. *5937 Geary Blvd., tel. 415/668–6654. Reservations advised. Dress: informal. AE, MC, V. No lunch. Closed Thanksgiving, Christmas, Labor Day. Inexpensive–Moderate.*

Steak Houses

Although San Francisco traditionally has not been a meat-and-potatoes town, the popularity of steak is on the rise. Following are some of the best steak houses, but you can also get a good piece of beef at some of the better French, Italian, and American restaurants.

Midtown **Harris'.** Ann Harris knows her beef. She grew
★ up on a Texas cattle ranch and was married to the late Jack Harris of Harris Ranch fame. In her own elegant restaurant she serves some of the best dry-aged steaks in town, but don't overlook the grilled seafood or poultry. Extensive bar menu. *2100 Van Ness Ave., tel. 415/673–1888. Reservations recommended. Dress: informal. AE, DC, MC, V. Lunch on Wed. only. Closed Christmas, New Year's Day. Valet parking. Expensive.*

Vegetarian

Aside from the restaurant mentioned below, vegetarians should also consider Gaylord's (*see* Indian restaurants, *above*), which offers a wide variety of meatless dishes from the Hindu cuisine.

Marina **Greens at Fort Mason.** This beautiful restaurant
★ with its bay views is a favorite with carnivores as well as vegetarians. Owned and operated by the Tassajara Zen Center of Carmel Valley, the restaurant offers a wide, eclectic, and creative spectrum of meatless cooking, and the bread promises nirvana. Dinners are à la carte on weeknights, but only a five-course prix-fixe dinner is served on Friday and Saturday. *Bldg. A, Fort Mason, tel. 415/771–6222. Dress: informal. Reservations advised. MC, V. No dinner Sun. Closed Mon., Thanksgiving, Christmas, New Year's Day. Public parking at Fort Mason Center. Moderate.*

5   Lodging

By Laura Del Rosso

Laura Del Rosso is San Francisco bureau chief for Travel Weekly, *a news magazine for the travel industry, and often writes about San Francisco for other publications.*

Few cities in the United States can rival San Francisco's variety in lodging. There are plush hotels ranked among the finest in the world, renovated older buildings that have the charm of Europe, bed-and-breakfast inns in the city's Victorian "Painted Ladies," and the popular chain hotels found in most cities in the United States.

One of the brightest spots in the lodging picture is the transformation of handsome early 20th-century downtown high rises into small, distinctive hotels that offer personal service and European-style ambience. Another is the recent addition of ultradeluxe modern hotels such as the Nikko, Pan Pacific, ANA, and Mandarin Oriental, which promote their attentive Asian-style hospitality. On top of those offerings are the dozens of popular chain hotels that continually undergo face-lifts and additions to keep up with the competition.

Because San Francisco is one of the top destinations in the United States for tourists as well as business travelers and convention goers, reservations are always advised, especially during the May–October peak season.

San Francisco's geography makes it conveniently compact. No matter their location, the hotels listed below are on or close to public transportation lines. Some properties on Lombard Street and in the Civic Center area have free parking, but a car is more a hindrance than an asset in San Francisco.

Although not as high as New York, San Francisco hotel prices may come as a surprise to travelers from less urban areas. Average rates for double rooms downtown and at the wharf are in the $110 range. Adding to the expense is the city's 11% transient occupancy tax, which can significantly boost the cost of a lengthy stay. The good news is that because of the hotel building boom of the late 1980s there is now an oversupply of rooms, which has led to much discounting of prices. Check for special rates and packages when making reservations.

An alternative to hotels and motels is staying in private homes and apartments, available

through **American F...**
San Francisco (Box ...
94142, tel. 415/931–3...
ternational–San Fra...
Ave., Albany, CA 947...
800/872–4500), and **A...**
change (170 Page St., Sa...
tel. 415/863–8484 or 800/...

The **San Francisco Conven...** ...isitors Bureau** (tel. 800/677–1550) publishes a free lodging guide with a map and listing of all hotels. Send $1 for postage and handling to Box 6977, San Francisco, CA 94101-6977. The bureau also arranges accommodations.

If you are looking for truly budget accommodations (under $50), consider the Adelaide Inn (*see* Union Square/Downtown, *below*) and the **YMCA Central Branch**. *220 Golden Gate Ave. 94102, tel. 415/885–0460. 102 rooms, 3 with bath. Facilities: health club, pool, sauna. MC, V.*

The most highly recommended hotels are indicated by a star ★.

Lodgings are listed by geographical area and price range.

Category	Cost*
Very Expensive	over $175
Expensive	$110–$175
Moderate	$75–$110
Inexpensive	under $75

**All prices are for a standard double room, excluding 11% tax.*

The following credit card abbreviations are used: AE, American Express; DC, Diners Club; MC, MasterCard; V, Visa.

Union Square/Downtown

The largest variety and greatest concentration of hotels are in the city's downtown hub, Union Square, where hotel guests find the best shopping, the theater district, and transportation to every spot in San Francisco.

Campton Place Kempinski. Steps away from Union Square is one of San Francisco's most elegant and highly rated hotels. Campton Place came under the management of the Kempinski organization, a German hotel company, in 1991. However, the attentive, personal service that begins from the moment uniformed doormen greet guests outside the marble-floor lobby has not changed. *340 Stockton St., 94108, tel. 415/ 781–5555; 800/647–4007; in CA, 800/235–4300. 126 rooms. Facilities: restaurant, bar. AE, DC, MC, V.*

★ **Four Seasons Clift.** Probably San Francisco's most acclaimed hotel, this stately landmark is the first choice of many celebrities and discriminating travelers for its attentive personal service. Special attention is given to children, with fresh cookies and milk provided at bedtime. All rooms are sumptuously decorated—the suites in elegant black and gray, others in bright beige and pink—in a somewhat updated contemporary style. *495 Geary St., 94102, tel. 415/775– 4700 or 800/332–3442. 329 rooms. Facilities: restaurant, Redwood Room lounge. AE, DC, MC, V.*

Grand Hyatt. This hotel overlooks Union Square and Ruth Asawa's fantasy fountain in the garden (*see* Tour 1: Union Square in Chapter 3). The hotel, formerly the Hyatt on Union Square, underwent a $20 million renovation in 1990. *345 Stockton St., 94108, tel. 415/398–1234 or 800/233–1234. 693 rooms. Facilities: 2 restaurants, 2 lounges, shopping arcade. AE, DC, MC, V.*

Hotel Nikko–San Francisco. Trickling waterfalls and walls of white marble set a quiet, subtle mood at this fine Japanese Airlines–owned hotel. The rooms are pink and gray contemporary with an Oriental touch. *222 Mason St., 94102, tel. 415/394–1111 or 800/645–5687. 525 rooms. Facilities: indoor pool, health club and spa, 2 restaurants, lounge. AE, DC, MC, V.*

San Francisco Hilton on Hilton Square. A huge expansion and renovation in 1988 made this by far the largest hotel in San Francisco. Popular with convention and tour groups. *1 Hilton Sq. (O'Farrell and Mason Sts.), tel. 415/771–1400 or 800/445–8667. 1,907 rooms. Facilities: 4 res-*

taurants, 2 lounges, pool, shopping arcade.
AE, DC, MC, V.

Westin St. Francis. This is one of the grand hotels of San Francisco and a Union Square landmark. Rooms in the original building have been
redecorated but still retain some of the 1904
moldings and bathroom tiles. Rooms in the modern tower have brighter, lacquered furniture.
In 1991 three 40-foot tromp l'oeil murals were
installed in the renovated tower lobby, and the
main lobby received new marble floors. *335 Powell St., 94102, tel. 415/397–7000 or 800/228–
3000. 1,200 rooms. Facilities: 5 restaurants, 5
lounges, shopping arcade. AE, DC, MC, V.*

Expensive   **Holiday Inn–Union Square.** This hotel enjoys a
good location on the cable car line only a block
from Union Square. The decor of the Sherlock
Holmes Lounge is 221-B Baker Street all the
way. *480 Sutter St., 94108, tel. 415/398–8900 or
800/465–4329. 400 rooms. Facilities: restaurant, lounge. AE, DC, MC, V.*

Hotel Diva. This hotel attracts the avant garde
set with a high-tech look that sets it apart from
any other hotel in San Francisco. *440 Geary St.,
94102, tel. 415/885–0200 or 800/553–1900. 125
rooms. Facilities: restaurant, lounge. AE, DC,
MC, V.*

Inn at Union Square. The individually decorated
rooms with goosedown pillows and four-poster
beds here are sumptuous. Continental breakfast and afternoon tea are served before a fireplace in the cozy sitting areas on each floor. *440
Post St., 04102, tel. 415/397–3510 or 800/288–
4346. 30 rooms. AE, DC, MC, V.*

Kensington Park. A handsome, high-ceilinged
lobby sets the mood of this fine hotel, where afternoon tea and sherry are served. The rooms
are decorated with English Queen Anne–style
furniture. *450 Post St., 94102, tel. 415/788–6400
or 800/553–1900. 90 rooms. AE, DC, MC, V.*

★ **Petite Auberge.** The French countryside was imported to downtown San Francisco to create this
charming bed-and-breakfast inn. Calico-printed
wallpaper, fluffy down comforters, and French
reproduction antiques decorate each room.
Most have wood-burning fireplaces. Next door
is the sister hotel, the 27-room **White Swan,** similar in style but with an English country flavor.

Downtown San Francisco Lodging

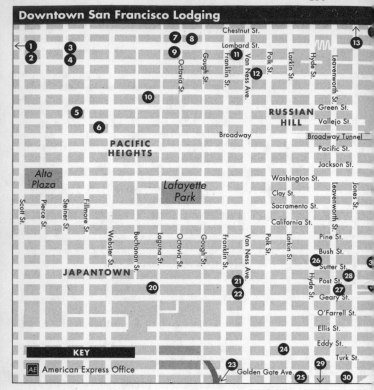

Abigail Hotel, **25**

Adelaide Inn, **31**

Amsterdam, **32**

The Bed and
Breakfast
Inn, **10**

Bel Aire
TraveLodge, **4**

Beresford
Arms, **28**

Best Western
Americania, **46**

Campton Place
Kempinski, **59**

The
Cartwright, **40**

Cathedral
Hill, **21**

Chancellor
Hotel, **54**

Columbus Motor
Inn, **14**

Cow Hollow
Motor Inn, **3**

Edward II, **2**

Fairmont, **37**

Four Seasons
Clift, **43**

Galleria Park, **65**

Grand Hyatt, **58**

Grant Plaza, **60**

Handlery
Hotel, **51**

Holiday Inn-
Civic Center, **29**

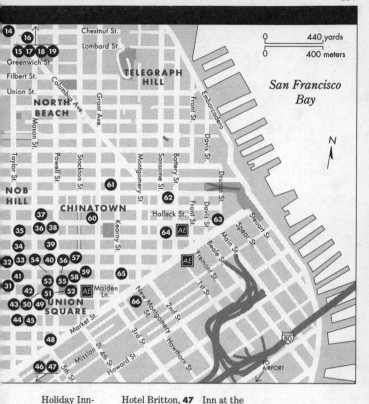

Downtown San Francisco Lodging

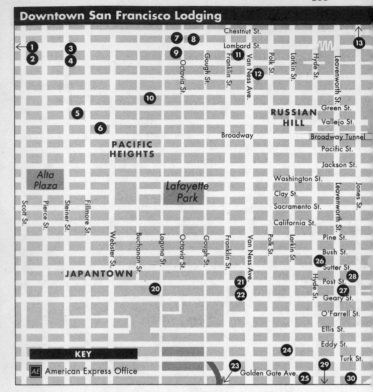

Marina Inn, **7**

Marina Motel, **1**

Mark Hopkins Inter-Continental, **36**

Miyako, **20**

Monticello Inn, **48**

The Park Hyatt, **62**

Petite Auberge, **33**

The Phoenix Inn, **24**

The Prescott Hotel, **41**

Ramada Hotel-Fisherman's Wharf, **13**

The Raphael, **50**

San Francisco Bay Motel, **11**

San Francisco Hilton on Hilton Square, **44**

San Francisco Marriott-Fisherman's Wharf, **15**

San Remo Hotel, **17**

Sheraton at Fisherman's Wharf, **18**

Sheraton Palace, **66**

The Sherman House, **6**

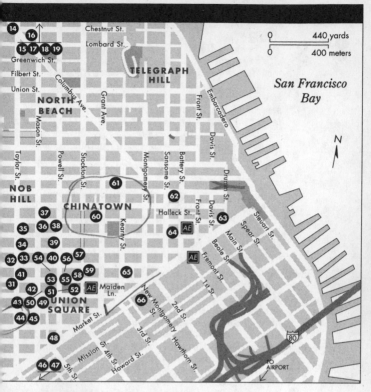

Sir Francis Drake, **56**	TraveLodge at the Wharf, **19**	Vintage Court, **39**
Star Motel, **9**	Union Street Inn, **5**	Westin St. Francis, **52**
Stouffer Stanford Court, **38**	U.N. Plaza Hotel, **30**	White Swan, **34**
Town House Motel, **8**	Vagabond Inn, **12**	York Hotel, **26**

845 Bush St., 94108, tel. 415/928–6000. 26 rooms. Facilities: breakfast rooms, parlors. AE, MC, V.

The Prescott Hotel. One of the plushest of the city's renovated old hotels, the Prescott may be most famous as home of Wolfgang Puck's Postrio restaurant. The hotel's emphasis is on personalized service, such as complimentary limousine service to the Financial District. *545 Post St., tel. 415/563–0303 or 800/283–7322. 167 rooms. Facilities: restaurant, lounge. AE, DC, MC, V.*

Sir Francis Drake. The rooms in this popular San Francisco hotel, famous for its Beefeater-costumed doormen, got a face-lift in 1986 during a multimillion-dollar renovation. They are decorated in an old English style, with mahogany furniture. The Starlight Roof is a lovely place for a drink. *450 Powell St., 94102, tel. 415/392–7755; 800/227–5480; in CA, 800/652–1668. nationwide. 415 rooms. Facilities: restaurant, lounge, exercise room. AE, DC, MC, V.*

Moderate **The Cartwright.** This is a family-owned hotel
★ with a friendly, personal touch in an ideal location. Renovated in 1986 after a five-year program to instill elegance and charm into the surroundings, this hotel offers rooms with brass or wood-carved beds, small refrigerators, and newly tiled bathrooms. *524 Sutter St., 94102, tel. 415/421–2865 or 800/227–3844. 114 rooms. Facilities: coffee shop open for breakfast. AE, DC, MC, V.*

★ **Chancellor Hotel.** This venerable hotel has been attracting a loyal clientele since it opened in 1924. Renovated in 1986, rooms have a new, elegant appearance with polished cherry-wood furniture. One of the best buys on Union Square. *433 Powell St., 94102, tel. 415/362–2004 or 800/428–4748. 140 rooms. Facilities: restaurant, lounge. AE, DC, MC, V.*

Galleria Park. This very attractive hotel is convenient to the Union Square shopping district. The guest rooms were all redecorated in late 1988 in a simplified French country style. *191 Sutter St., 94104, tel. 415/781–3060; 800/792–9636; in CA, 800/792–9855. 177 rooms. Facilities: rooftop park and jogging track, 2 restaurants, lounge. AE, DC, MC, V.*

Handlery Union Square Hotel. The former

Handlery Motor Inn and Stewart Hotel were combined and refurbished at a cost of $5 million in early 1988. The suitelike Handlery Club rooms are larger and more expensive. *351 Geary St., 94102, tel. 415/781–7800 or 800/223–0888. 378 rooms. Facilities: restaurant, outdoor heated pool, nonsmoking rooms. AE, DC, MC, V.*

Holiday Inn–Financial District. This hotel boasts an excellent location in Chinatown and is five minutes from Union Square and North Beach. Rooms on the 12th floor and above have city and bay views. *750 Kearny St., 94108, tel. 415/433–6600 or 800/465–4329. 556 rooms. Facilities: pool, restaurant, lounge, free parking. AE, DC, MC, V.*

Hotel Bedford. Big, cheery floral prints dominate the renovated guest rooms in this hotel, four blocks from Union Square. *761 Post St., 94109, tel. 415/673–6040; 800/227–5642; in CA, 800/652–1889. 144 rooms. Facilities: restaurant, English-style pub, in-room movie rentals. AE, DC, MC, V.*

★ **King George.** This charming midsize hotel was renovated in 1988 and 1989 to give it a more elegant, sophisticated look. The hotel's quaint Bread and Honey Tearoom serves traditional afternoon high tea. *334 Mason St., 94102, tel. 415/781–5050 or 800/288–6005. 144 rooms. Facilities: tearoom, lounge. AE, DC, MC, V.*

Monticello Inn. This hotel could boast "George Washington slept here" and most people would believe it. A little bit of the American Colonial period in the middle of downtown. Opened in 1987 after a complete renovation. The popular Corona Bar and Grill is off the lobby. *80 Cyril Magnin St., 94102, tel. 415/392–8800 or 800/669–7777. 91 rooms. Facilities: restaurant. AE, DC, MC, V.*

The Raphael. A favorite among repeat visitors to San Francisco, the Raphael was one of the first moderately priced European-style hotels in the city. Rooms were redecorated in 1988. The location is excellent. *386 Geary St., 94102, tel. 415/986–2000 or 800/821–5343. 151 rooms. Facilities: restaurant, lounge, in-room HBO. AE, DC, MC, V.*

Vintage Court. Beautifully furnished, elegant rooms, which were redecorated in 1989 in a

Wine Country theme, are featured. Complimentary wine is served before a crackling fire in the lobby in afternoons. *650 Bush St., 94108, tel. 415/392-4666; 800/654-1100; in CA, 800/654-7266. 106 rooms. Facilities: Masa's restaurant, lounge. AE, DC, MC, V.*

York Hotel. This very attractive, renovated old hotel is known for its Plush Room cabaret and as the site of a scene in Alfred Hitchcock's *Vertigo*. *940 Sutter St., 94109, tel. 415/885-6800 or 800/227-3608. 96 rooms. Facilities: nightclub, fitness center, complimentary chauffeured limousine. AE, DC, MC, V.*

Inexpensive **Adelaide Inn.** The bedspreads may not match the drapes or carpets and the floors may creak, but the rooms are clean and cheap (less than $50 for a double room) at this friendly small hotel that is popular with Europeans. Continental breakfast is complimentary. *5 Isadora Duncan Ct. (off Taylor between Geary and Post), 94102, tel. 415/441-2474. 16 rooms, all share bath. Facilities: sitting room, refrigerator for guest use. AE, MC, V.*

Amsterdam. This European-style pension is in a Victorian building two blocks from Nob Hill. Rooms were renovated in 1988. *749 Taylor St., 94108, tel. 415/673-3277 or 800/637-3444. 30 rooms, 8 with shared bath. Facilities: cable TV in rooms, reading room, breakfast room for complimentary breakfast. AE, MC, V.*

Beresford Arms. Complimentary pastries and coffee are served in the hotel's grand old lobby. The suites with full kitchens are a good bargain for families. Standard rooms contain queen-size beds and small refrigerators. *701 Post St., 94109, tel. 415/673-2600 or 800/533-6533. 90 rooms. Facilities: some rooms have whirlpool baths. AE, DC, MC, V.*

★ **Grant Plaza.** This bargain-price hotel at the entrance of Chinatown has small but clean and attractively furnished rooms. No restaurant, but plenty of dining nearby. *465 Grant Ave., 94103, tel. 415/434-3883; 800/472-6899; in CA, 800/472-6805. 72 rooms. AE, MC, V.*

Aston Pickwick Hotel. A renovation in 1991 dramatically upgraded the rooms in this tourist-class hotel across from the San Francisco Mint and a block from the cable car turnaround.

Rooms are clean and attractively furnished, and have in-room voice mail. *85 5th St. at Mission, 94103, tel. 415/421–7500 or 800/922–7866. 189 rooms. Facilities: cocktail lounge, coffee shop, parking. AE, MC, V.*

Financial District

High-rise growth in San Francisco's Financial District has turned it into mini-Manhattan, a spectacular sight by night.

Very Expensive **Mandarin Oriental.** The third-highest building in San Francisco's skyline is topped by a luxurious 11-story hotel on its 38th–48th floors. It's the best for spectacular views, especially from the bathrooms in the Mandarin rooms with their floor-to-ceiling windows flanking the tubs. *222 Sansome St., 94104, tel. 415/885–0999 or 800/ 622–0404. 160 rooms. Facilities: gourmet restaurant, lounge. AE, DC, MC, V.*

Park Hyatt. This is the Hyatt chain's candidate for competing with the ultraluxury of some of the city's best hotels. Service is highly personal and attentive and rooms are plush, with such goodies as gourmet chocolates and imported soaps. Many rooms have balconies and bay views. The hotel caters to corporate executives and the like. *333 Battery St., tel. 415/392–1234 or 800/323–7275. 360 rooms. Facilities: restaurant, lounge, library room. AE, DC, MC, V.*

Expensive **Sheraton Palace.** One of the city's grand old hotels, the Sheraton reopened in 1991 after a $150 million reconstruction. New features include air-conditioning, a business center, health club, and pool. Happily, the Garden Court restaurant, famous for its leaded-glass ceiling, and the Pied Piper lounge, featuring Maxfield Parrish's painting of that name, were restored. *2 New Montgomery St., 94105, tel. 415/392–8600 or 800/325–3535. 550 rooms. Facilities: 24-hour room service, 2 restaurants, 2 lounges, fitness center. AE, DC, MC, V.*

Nob Hill

Synonymous with San Francisco's high society, Nob Hill contains some of the city's best-known luxury hotels. All offer spectacular city and bay views and noted gourmet restaurants. Cable car lines that cross Nob Hill make transportation a cinch.

Very Expensive **Fairmont Hotel and Tower.** The regal "grande dame" of Nob Hill, the Fairmont has one of the most spectacular lobbies and public rooms in the city. All guest rooms are spacious and finely decorated. Those in the modern tower have the best views, while those in the old building have the stately ambience of another era. *950 Mason St., 94108, tel. 415/772–5000 or 800/527–4727. 596 rooms. Facilities: health club and spa, gift shops, 5 restaurants, 5 lounges, 24-hour room service. AE, DC, MC, V.*

★ **Huntington Hotel.** Understated class is found in this little jewel atop Nob Hill. Sumptuous rooms and suites are individually decorated. *1075 California St., 94108, tel. 415/474–5400; worldwide, 800/227–4683; in CA, 800/652–1539. 143 rooms. Facilities: restaurant, lounge with entertainment. AE, DC, MC, V.*

Mark Hopkins Inter-Continental. Another Nob Hill landmark, "The Mark" is lovingly maintained. Rooms were redone in late 1987 in dramatic neoclassical furnishings of gray, silver, and khaki and with bold leaf-print bedspreads. Bathrooms are lined with Italian marble. Even-numbered rooms have views of the Golden Gate Bridge. *999 California St., 94108, tel. 415/392–3434 or 800/327–0200. 392 rooms. Facilities: gift shops, restaurant, lobby lounge, Top of the Mark cocktail lounge with panoramic views. AE, DC, MC, V.*

Stouffer Stanford Court Hotel. Since taking over three years ago, Stouffer has spent $10 million upgrading this acclaimed hotel. In 1992, a dramatic mural depicting scenes of early San Francisco was installed in the lobby under the lovely stained-glass dome. One of the city's finest restaurants, Fournou's Ovens, is located here. *905 California St., 94108, tel. 415/989–3500 or 800/227–4726. 402 rooms. Facilities: gift shops, 2 restaurants, 2 lounges. AE, DC, MC, V.*

Fisherman's Wharf/North Beach

Fisherman's Wharf, San Francisco's top tourist attraction, is also the most popular area for accommodations. All are within a couple of blocks of restaurants, shops, and cable car lines. Because of city ordinances, none of the hotels exceed four stories; thus, this is not the area for fantastic views of the city or bay. Reservations are always necessary, sometimes weeks in advance during the peak summer months (when hotel rates rise by as much as 30%). Some streetside rooms can be noisy.

Very Expensive

San Francisco Marriott–Fisherman's Wharf. Elegant lobby and guest rooms set the mood in one of the wharf's newest and finest hotels. *1250 Columbus Ave., 94133, tel. 415/775–7555 or 800/ 228–9290. 256 rooms. Facilities: restaurant, lounge, gift shop. AE, DC, MC, V.*

Expensive

Holiday Inn–Fisherman's Wharf. This large brick-faced hotel covers nearly two square blocks, including the 1984 addition, which has its own lobby and restaurant. Ongoing renovations keep rooms throughout the hotel upgraded. Charley's restaurant in the main building serves three excellent buffets; lunch brims with fresh seafood. *1300 Columbus Ave., 94133, tel. 415/771–9000 or 800/465–4329. 580 rooms. Facilities: outdoor pool, laundry rooms. AE, DC, MC, V.*

Ramada Hotel–Fisherman's Wharf. The well-appointed public areas and guest rooms have all been renovated within the past few years. *590 Bay St., 94133, tel. 415/885–4700 or 800/228– 8408. 231 rooms. Facilities: parking, running track, Parcourse. AE, DC, MC, V.*

Sheraton at Fisherman's Wharf. Rooms and corridors were handsomely refurnished in 1987 at this sprawling full-service hotel. Streetside rooms can be noisy; interior courtyard rooms are the quietest. *2500 Mason St., 94133, tel. 415/ 362–5500 or 800/325–3535. 525 rooms. Facilities: outdoor pool, restaurant, cocktail lounge. AE, DC, MC, V.*

Moderate

Columbus Motor Inn. This is an attractive motel between the wharf and North Beach with suites that are ideal for families. *1075 Columbus Ave., 94133, tel. 415/885–1492. 45 rooms. Facilities: free parking. AE, DC, MC, V.*

TraveLodge at the Wharf. This is an attractive hotel whose rooms were tastefully redecorated during the past few years. Higher priced interior rooms (third and fourth floors) have balconies overlooking the landscaped deck and swimming pool, as well as unobstructed views of Alcatraz. *250 Beach St., 94133, tel. 415/392–6700 or 800/ 255–3050. 250 rooms. Facilities: outdoor pool, restaurant, lounge, free parking. AE, DC, MC, V.*

Inexpensive **San Remo Hotel.** This cozy hotel is reminiscent
★ of a European-style pension. Renovated during recent years, its smallish rooms and narrow corridors are freshly painted and decorated with plants and antiques. It offers a good location on the border of Fisherman's Wharf and North Beach. *2237 Mason St., 94133, tel. 415/776– 8688. 62 rooms, all with shared baths. Daily and weekly rates. Facilities: popular Italian restaurant. AE, DC, MC, V.*

Lombard Street/Cow Hollow

Lombard Street, a major traffic corridor leading to the Golden Gate Bridge, is sandwiched between two of San Francisco's poshest neighborhoods, Cow Hollow and the Marina District.

Very **The Sherman House.** In the middle of an elegant
Expensive residential district is this magnificent landmark
★ mansion, the most luxurious small hotel in San Francisco. Each room is individually decorated with Biedermeier, English Jacobean, or French Second-Empire antiques, with tapestrylike canopies covering four-poster beds. Marble-top, wood-burning fireplaces and black granite bathrooms with whirlpool baths complete the picture. There is an in-house restaurant for guests only. *2160 Green St., 94123, tel. 415/563–3600. 15 rooms. Facilities: dining room, sitting rooms. AE, DC, MC, V.*

Moderate **The Bed and Breakfast Inn.** The first of San Francisco's B&Bs, this is an ivy-covered renovated Victorian located in an alleyway off Union Street. Romantic, cheery rooms with flowery wallpaper include "The Mayfair," a flat with a spiral staircase leading to a sleeping loft. Some rooms are more modest and share baths. *4 Charlton Ct., 94123, tel. 415/921–9784. 10 rooms with baths. Facilities: breakfast room. No credit cards.*
Bel Aire TraveLodge. This attractive, well-kept motel is in a quiet location half a block from

Lombard Street. *3201 Steiner St., 94123, tel. 415/921–5162 or 800/255–3050. 32 rooms. Facilities: free parking. AE, DC, MC, V.*

Cow Hollow Motor Inn. This is a large, modern motel with lovely rooms that were all renovated in 1988 with thick, new burgundy carpeting and rose-colored bedspreads. *2190 Lombard St., 94123, tel. 415/921–5800. 129 rooms. Facilities: restaurant, free parking. AE, DC, MC, V.*

★ **Marina Inn.** Here cute B&B-style accommodations are offered at motel prices. Dainty-flowered wallpaper, poster beds, country pine furniture, and fresh flowers give the rooms an English country air. Continental breakfast is served in the cozy central sitting room. Turned-down beds and chocolates greet guests at the end of the day. No parking. *3110 Octavia St. at Lombard St., 94123, tel. 415/928–1000. 40 rooms. Facilities: lounge. AE, MC, V.*

Union Street Inn. A retired schoolteacher has transformed this 1902 Edwardian home into a cozy inn. Antiques and fresh flowers are found throughout. *2229 Union St., 94123, tel. 415/346–0424. 6 rooms with private bath. Facilities: English garden, breakfast room. AE, MC, V.*

Vagabond Inn. This is a beautifully maintained motor inn that overlooks a central courtyard swimming pool. Some fourth- and fifth-floor rooms have views of the Golden Gate Bridge. *2550 Van Ness Ave. near Lombard St., 94109, tel. 415/776–7500 or 800/522–1555 in CA. 132 rooms. Facilities: outdoor pool, 24-hour restaurant, lounge. AE, DC, MC, V.*

Inexpensive **Edward II Inn.** Standard rooms are smallish and parking is not available, but reasonable prices and a quaint pension atmosphere offset these drawbacks. *3155 Scott St. at Lombard St., 94123, tel. 415/922–3000. 30 rooms, 14 with bath. Facilities: restaurant. AE, MC, V.*

Marina Motel. This quaint Spanish-style stucco complex is one of the oldest motels on Lombard Street, but it is well kept. Each room has its own garage. *2576 Lombard St., 94123, tel. 415/921–9406. 45 rooms, some with kitchen. Facilities: free parking. AE, MC, V.*

Star Motel. This is a well-maintained motel with basic rooms. *1727 Lombard St., 94123, tel. 415/*

346–8250 or 800/835–8143. 52 rooms. Facilities: free parking. AE, DC, MC, V.

★ **Town House Motel.** A very attractive motel with recently redecorated rooms, this is one of the best values on Lombard Street. *1650 Lombard St., 94123, tel. 415/885–5163 or 800/255–1516. 24 rooms. Facilities: free parking. AE, DC, MC, V.*

Civic Center/Van Ness

The governmental heart of San Francisco has been undergoing a renaissance that has made it come alive with fine restaurants, trendy night spots, and renovated small hotels.

Expensive **Cathedral Hill Hotel.** Guest rooms were renovated in 1988 at this popular convention hotel. *1101 Van Ness Ave., 94109, tel. 415/776–8200; 800/227–4730; in CA, 800/622–0855. 400 rooms. Facilities: free parking, pool, 2 restaurants, lounge. AE, DC, MC, V.*

★ **Inn at the Opera.** A music or ballet lover's heart may quiver at the sight of this lovely small hotel, where musicians and singers stay when they appear at San Francisco's performing arts centers a block away. There are billowing pillows, terry-cloth robes, microwave ovens, and servibars in each room. *333 Fulton St., 94102, tel. 415/863–8400; 800/325–2708; in CA, 800/ 423–9610. 48 rooms. Facilities: restaurant, lounge. AE, DC, MC, V.*

Miyako. In the heart of Japantown is this elegant, recently renovated hotel. The Japanese ambience is established by a greeting from a kimono-clad hostess. Traditional Japanese rooms with tatami mats are available. *1625 Post St. at Laguna St., 94115, tel. 415/922–3200 or 800/ 533–4567. 218 rooms. Facilities: Japanese baths, saunas, restaurant, 2 lounges. AE, DC, MC, V.*

Moderate **Abigail Hotel.** A former B&B inn, this hotel re-
★ tains its homey atmosphere with an eclectic mix of English antiques and mounted hunting trophies in the lobby. Hissing steam radiators and sleigh beds set the mood in the antiques-filled rooms. Room 211—the hotel's only suite—is the most elegant and spacious. *246 McAllister St.,*

94102, tel. 415/861–9728 or 800/243–6510. 62 rooms. AE, DC, MC, V.

Best Western Americania. This hotel is distinguished by its pink-and-turquoise Moorish facade. Rooms overlook inner courtyards with fountain or swimming pool. *121 7th St., 94103, tel. 415/626–0200 or 800/444–5816. 142 rooms. Facilities: outdoor pool, sauna, coffee shop, free parking, nonsmoking rooms available, evening shuttle to Union Square. AE, DC, MC, V.*

Holiday Inn–Civic Center. A 1989 renovation of the exterior, all rooms, lobby, and the restaurant has added a touch of elegance. The location is good—three blocks from the Civic Center and two blocks from Brooks Hall/Civic Auditorium. *50 8th St., 94103, tel. 415/626–6103 or 800/465–4329. 390 rooms. Facilities: restaurant, lounge, outdoor pool. AE, DC, MC, V.*

★ **Lombard Hotel.** This is a European-style hotel with a handsome marble-floor lobby flanked on one side by the Gray Derby restaurant. Many of the rooms were refurbished in 1989 with blondwood furniture and new servibars. Quiet rooms are in the back. Complimentary evening cocktails and chauffeured limousine downtown are offered. *1015 Geary St., 94109, tel. 415/673–5232 or 800/227–3608. 100 rooms. Facilities: restaurant. AE, DC, MC, V.*

The Phoenix Inn. Resembling more of a '50s-style beachside resort than a hotel in San Francisco's government center, the Phoenix bills itself aptly as an "urban retreat." Bungalow-style rooms, decorated with casual Filipino bamboo and original art by San Francisco artists, all face a pool courtyard and sculpture garden. *601 Eddy St., 94109, tel. 415/776–1380. 44 rooms. Facilities: free parking, lounge, heated pool. AE, DC, MC, V.*

Inexpensive **Hotel Britton.** This hotel is clean and comfort-
★ able, with good rates, and is close to the Civic Center. Rooms are attractively furnished, and color TVs offer in-room movies. *112 7th St. at Mission St., 94103, tel. 415/621–7001 or 800/444–5819. 80 rooms. Facilities: coffee shop. AE, DC, MC, V.*

6 The Arts and Nightlife

The Arts

By Robert Taylor

Longtime San Franciscan Robert Taylor writes about the arts for the Oakland *Tribune.*

The best guide to arts and entertainment events in San Francisco is the "Datebook" section, printed on pink paper, in the Sunday *Examiner and Chronicle.* The *Bay Guardian* and *S.F. Weekly*, free and available in racks around the city, list more neighborhood, avant-garde, and budget-priced events. For up-to-date information about cultural and musical events, call the Convention and Visitors Bureau's *Cultural Events Calendar* (tel. 415/391–2001).

Half-price tickets to many local and touring stage shows go on sale (cash only) at noon Tuesday–Saturday at the **STBS** booth on the Stockton Street side of Union Square, between Geary and Post streets. STBS is also a full-service ticket agency for theater and music events around the Bay Area (open until 7:30 PM). While the city's major commercial theaters are concentrated downtown, the opera, symphony, and ballet perform at the Civic Center. For recorded information about STBS tickets, call 415/433–7827.

The city's charge-by-phone ticket service is **BASS** (tel. 415/762–2277), with one of its centers in the STBS booth mentioned above and another at **Tower Records** (Bay St. at Columbus Ave.), near Fisherman's Wharf. Other agencies downtown are the **City Box Office**, 141 Kearny Street in the Sherman-Clay store (tel. 415/392–4400) and **Downtown Center Box Office** in the parking garage at 320 Mason Street (tel. 415/775–2021). The opera, symphony, the ballet's *Nutcracker*, and touring hit musicals are often sold out in advance; tickets are usually available within a day of performance for other shows.

Theater

San Francisco's "theater row" is a single block of Geary Street west of Union Square, but a number of commercial theaters are located within walking distance, along with resident companies that enrich the city's theatrical scene. The three major commercial theaters are operated by the Shorenstein-Nederlander organization, which books touring plays and musicals, some of them before they open on Broadway. The most

venerable is the **Curran** (445 Geary St., tel. 415/
673–4400), which is used for plays and smaller
musicals. The **Golden Gate** is a stylishly refurbished movie theater (Golden Gate Ave. at Taylor St., tel. 415/474–3800), primarily a musical
house. The 2,500-seat **Orpheum** (1192 Market
St. near the Civic Center, tel. 415/474–3800) is
used for the biggest touring shows.

The smaller commercial theaters, offering touring shows and a few that are locally produced,
are the **Marines Memorial Theatre** (Sutter and
Mason Sts., tel. 415/441–7444) and **Theatre on
the Square** (450 Post St., tel. 415/433–9500). For
commercial and popular success, nothing beats
*Beach Blanket Babylon,*the zany revue that has
been running for years at **Club Fugazi** (678
Green St. in North Beach, tel. 415/421–4222).
Conceived by imaginative San Francisco director Steve Silver, it is a lively, colorful musical
mix of cabaret, show-biz parodies, and tributes
to local landmarks. (*See* Cabarets in Nightlife,
below.) The city's major theater company is the
American Conservatory Theatre (ACT), which
quickly became one of the nation's leading regional theaters when it was founded during the
mid-1960s. It presents a season of approximately eight plays in rotating repertory from October through late spring. The ACT's ticket office
is at the **Geary Theatre** (415 Geary St., tel. 415/
749–2228), though the theater itself was closed
following the 1989 earthquake. During recon-
struction ACT is performing at the nearby **Stage
Door Theater** (420 Mason St.) and the **Theatre on
the Square** (450 Post St.).

At the next level are several established theaters in smaller houses and with lower ticket
prices that specialize in contemporary plays.
The most reliable are the **Eureka Theatre** (2730
16th St. in the Mission District, tel. 415/558–
9898) and the **Magic Theatre** (Bldg. D, Fort Mason Center, Laguna St. at Marina Blvd., tel.
415/441–8822).

The city boasts a wide variety of specialized and
ethnic theaters that work with dedicated local
actors and some professionals. Among the most
interesting are **The Lamplighters**, the delightful
Gilbert and Sullivan troupe that often gets bet-

ter reviews than touring productions of musicals, performing at **Presentation Theater** (2350 Turk St., tel. 415/752–7755); the **Lorraine Hansberry Theatre**, which specializes in plays by black writers (620 Sutter St., tel. 415/474–8800); the **Asian American Theatre** (405 Arguello Blvd., tel. 415/346–8922); and the gay and lesbian **Theatre Rhinoceros** (2926 16th St., tel. 415/861–5079). The **San Francisco Shakespeare Festival** offers free performances on summer weekends in Golden Gate Park (tel. 415/221–0642).

Avant-garde theater, dance, opera, and "performance art" turn up in a variety of locations, not all of them theaters. The major presenting organizations are **Life on the Water** (Bldg. B, Fort Mason Center, Laguna St. at Marina Blvd., tel. 415/776–8999) and **Theater Artaud** (499 Alabama St. in the Mission District, tel. 415/621–7797) in a huge, converted machine shop. One more trendy performance center is the **Climate** theater (252 9th St., tel. 415/626–9196), in the neighborhood of the newest cafés, clubs, and galleries.

Berkeley Repertory Theatre across the bay is the American Conservatory Theatre's major rival for leadership among the region's resident professional companies. It performs a more adventurous mix of classics and new plays in a more modern, intimate theater at 2025 Addison Street near BART's downtown Berkeley station (tel. 510/845–4700). It's a fully professional theater, with a fall–spring season and special events during the summer. Tickets are available at the STBS booth in San Francisco's Union Square. The Bay Area's most professional outdoor summer theater, **California Shakespeare Festival**, has moved from Berkeley to a new amphitheater east of Oakland, on Gateway Boulevard just off state Highway 24 (tel. 510/548–3422).

Music

The completion of Davies Symphony Hall at Van Ness Avenue and Grove Street finally gave the San Francisco Symphony a home of its own. It solidified the base of the city's three major performing arts organizations—symphony, opera,

and ballet—in the Civic Center. The symphony
and other musical groups also perform in the
smaller, 928-seat Herbst Theatre in the Opera's
"twin" at Van Ness Avenue and McAllister
Street, the War Memorial Building. Otherwise
the city's musical ensembles can be found all
over the map: in churches and museums, in restaurants and outdoors in parks, and in outreach
series in Berkeley and on the peninsula.

San Francisco Symphony (Davies Symphony
Hall, Van Ness Ave. at Grove St., tel. 415/431–
5400. Tickets at the box office or through BASS,
tel. 415/762–2277). The city's most stable performing arts organization plays from September through May, with music director Herbert
Blomstedt conducting for about two-thirds of
the season. Guest conductors often include Michael Tilson Thomas, Edo de Waart, and
Riccardo Mutti. Guest soloists include artists of
the caliber of Andre Watts, Leontyne Price, and
Jean-Pierre Rampal. The symphony has stayed
with the standard repertoire in recent years as
Blomstedt concentrates on the ensemble's sta-
bility and focus. Special events include a Mostly
Mozart festival during the spring, a Beethoven
festival during the summer, a New and Unusual
Music series during the spring in the more intimate Herbst Theatre, and summer Pops Concerts in the nearby Civic Auditorium.
Throughout the season, the symphony presents
a Great Performers Series of guest soloists and
orchestras.
Philharmonia Baroque (Herbst Theatre, Van
Ness Ave. at McAllister St., tel. 415/552–3656.
Tickets also at STBS booth in Union Square).
This stylish ensemble has been called the local
baroque orchestra with the national reputation.
Its season of concerts, fall–spring, celebrates
composers of the 17th and 18th centuries, including Handel, Vivaldi, and Mozart.
Chamber Symphony of San Francisco (various
locations, tel. 415/441–4636). Under musical director Jean-Louis Le Roux, this group has become known for the variety of its programming,
which can include composers from Handel to
VillaLobos.
Kronos Quartet (Herbst Theatre and other locations, tel. 415/731–3533). Twentieth-century

works and a number of premieres make up the programs for this group that goes as far as possible to prove that string quartets are not stodgy.

Midsummer Mozart (Herbst Theatre and occasionally at Davies Symphony Hall, tel. 415/781–5931). This is one of the few Mozart festivals that hasn't filled programs with works by other composers. It performs in July and August under George Cleve, conductor of the San Jose Symphony.

Old First Concerts (Old First Church, Van Ness Ave. at Sacramento St., tel. 415/474–1608. Tickets also at STBS booth, Union Square). This is a well-respected Friday evening and Sunday afternoon series of chamber music, vocal soloists, new music, and jazz.

Pops Concerts (Polk and Grove Sts., tel. 415/431–5400). Many members of the symphony perform in the July pops series in the 7,000-seat Civic Auditorium. The schedule includes light classics, Broadway, country, and movie music. Tickets cost as little as a few dollars.

Stern Grove (Sloat Blvd. at 19th Ave., tel. 415/398–6551). This is the nation's oldest continual free summer music festival, offering 10 Sunday afternoons of symphony, opera, jazz, pop music, and dance. The amphitheater is in a eucalyptus grove below street level; remember that summer in this area near the ocean can be cool.

There are also free band concerts on Sunday and holiday afternoons in the Golden Gate Park music concourse (tel. 415/558–3706) opposite the de Young Museum.

Opera

San Francisco Opera (Van Ness Ave. at Grove St., tel. 415/864–3330). Founded in 1923, and the resident company at the War Memorial Opera House in the Civic Center since it was built in 1932, the Opera has expanded to a fall season of 13 weeks. Approximately 70 performances of 10 operas are given, beginning on the first Friday after Labor Day. For many years the Opera was considered a major international company and the most artistically successful operatic organization in the United States. International competition and management changes have made recent seasons uneven; the company has revitalized under general director Lofti Mansouri, formerly head of Toronto's Canadian Opera Company. International opera stars frequently sing major roles here, but the Opera is also well known for presenting the American debuts of singers who have made their name in Europe. In the same way, the company's standard repertoire is interspersed with revivals of rarely heard works.

The Opera was one of the first to present "supertitles," projecting English translations above the stage during performances. The system is used for almost all operas not sung in English. In addition to the fall season, the Opera performs Wagner's Ring cycle every five summers—next in 1995. Ticket prices range from about $28 to a high of about $90, and many performances are sold out far in advance. Standing-room tickets are always sold, however, and patrons often sell extra tickets on the Opera House steps just before curtain time.

Pocket Opera (tel. 415/346–2780). This lively, modestly priced alternative to "grand" opera gives concert performances, mostly in English, of rarely heard works. Offenbach's operettas are frequently on the bill during the winter-spring season. Concerts are held at various locations.

Another operatic alternative is the **Lamplighters** (*see* Theater, *above*), which specializes in Gilbert and Sullivan but presents other light operas as well.

Dance

San Francisco Ballet (War Memorial Opera House, Van Ness Ave. at Grove St., tel. 415/621–3838). The ballet has regained much of its luster under artistic director Helgi Tomasson, and both classical and contemporary works have won admiring reviews. The company's primary season runs February–May; its repertoire includes such full-length ballets as *Swan Lake* and a new production of *Sleeping Beauty*. The company is also intent on reaching new audiences with bold new dances, what it likes to call "cutting-edge works that will make you take a second look." Like many dance companies in the nation, the ballet presents *The Nutcracker* in December, and its recent production is one of the most spectacular.

Oakland Ballet (Paramount Theatre, 2025 Broadway, Oakland, near BART's 19th St. station, tel. 510/452–9288). Founded in 1965, this company is not simply an imitation of the larger San Francisco Ballet across the bay. It has earned an outstanding reputation for reviving and preserving ballet masterworks from the early 20th century and presenting innovative contemporary choreography. It has re-created historic dances by such choreographers as Diaghilev, Bronislava Nininska, and Mikhail Fokine. The company also presents its own *Nutcracker* in December; its season begins in September.

Margaret Jenkins Dance Company (Theater Artaud, 450 Florida St., tel. 415/863–1173). This is one of the most reliable of the city's modern experimental dance troupes, in which the dancers themselves help shape the choreography.

Ethnic Dance Festival (Palace of Fine Arts Theatre, Bay and Lyon Sts., tel. 415/474–3914). Approximately 30 of the Bay Area's estimated 200 ethnic dance companies and soloists perform on several programs in June. Prices are modest for the city-sponsored event.

San Francisco and the Bay Area support innumerable experimental and ethnic dance groups. Among them are **ODC/San Francisco** (tel. 415/863–6606), performing at Herbst Theatre (Van Ness Ave.); the **Joe Goode Performance Group** (tel. 415/648–4848); **Kulintang Arts,** (tel. 415/553–8824), a Philippine troupe; and **Rosa Montoya Bailes Flamenco** (tel. 415/931–7374), which often performs at Herbst Theatre.

Film

The San Francisco Bay Area, including Berkeley and San Jose, is considered to be one of the nation's most important movie markets. If there is a film floating around the country or around the world in search of an audience, it is likely that it will eventually turn up on a screen in San

Francisco. The Bay Area is also a filmmaking center: Documentaries and experimental works are being produced on modest budgets, feature films and television programs are shot on location, and some of Hollywood's biggest directors prefer to live here, particularly in Marin County. In San Francisco, about a third of the theaters regularly show foreign and independent films. The city is also one of the last strongholds of "repertory cinema," showing older American and foreign films on bills that change daily.

San Francisco's traditional movie theater center, downtown on Market Street, is pretty much given over to sex and action movies nowadays. First-run commercial movie theaters are now scattered throughout the city, although they are concentrated along Van Ness Avenue, near Japantown, and in the Marina District. All are accessible on major Muni bus routes, as are the art-revival houses. Several of the most respected and popular independent theaters have been taken over by chains recently, and their policy could change. The San Francisco International Film Festival (*see below*), the oldest in the country, continues to provide an extensive selection of foreign films each spring. The Pacific Film Archive in Berkeley (*see below*) is an incomparable source for rare American and foreign films.

Foreign and Independent Films The most reliable theaters for foreign and independent films are **Opera Plaza Cinemas** (Van Ness Ave. at Golden Gate Ave., tel. 415/771–0102); **Lumiere** (California St. near Polk St., tel. 415/885–3200); **Clay** (Fillmore and Clay Sts., tel. 415/346–1123); **Gateway** (215 Jackson St. at Battery St., tel. 415/421–3353); **Castro** (Castro St. near Market St., tel. 415/621–6120), the last remaining movie palace from the 1920s that is still showing movies, with an extensive schedule of revivals; and **Bridge** (3013 Geary Blvd. near Masonic Ave., tel. 415/751–3212).

Festivals **The San Francisco International Film Festival** (tel. 415/931–3456) takes over several theaters for two weeks in late March at the AMC Kabuki complex at Post and Fillmore streets. The festival schedules about 75 films from abroad, many of them American premieres, along with a variety of independent American documentaries. During recent years there has been an emphasis on films from Africa and Asia.

Other showcases for films out of the commercial mainstream include **The Roxie** (3116 16th St., tel. 415/863–1087), which specializes in social and political documentaries; the **Cinematheque** at the San Francisco Art Institute (800 Chestnut St., tel. 415/558–8129), which often features films by avant-garde artists; and **Eye Gallery** (1151 Mission St., tel. 415/431–6911), which offers experimental videos and films.

The most extensive screening schedule for both American and foreign, old and new films is the **Pacific Film Archive** (2625 Durant Ave., Berkeley, tel. 510/642–1124). It often shows films from New York's Museum of Modern Art collection.

Nightlife

By Dan Spitzer

A Bay Area resident, Dan Spitzer has written travel books about South America and the Far East.

San Francisco provides a tremendous potpourri of evening entertainment ranging from ultrasophisticated cabarets to bawdy bistros that reflect the city's gold rush past. With the exception of the hotel lounges and discos noted below, the accent is on casual dress—call ahead if you are uncertain.

For information on who is performing where, check the following sources: The Sunday San Francisco *Examiner and Chronicle*'s pink "Datebook" insert lists major events and cultural happenings. The free alternative weekly, the *Bay Guardian*, is a terrific source for current music clubs and comedy. Another handy reference for San Francisco nightlife is *Key* magazine, offered free in most major hotel lobbies. For a phone update on sports and musical events, call the Convention and Visitor Bureau's *Cultural Events Calendar* (tel. 415/391–2001). Those seeking weekly jazz headliners should dial the KJAZ *Jazz Line* (tel. 510/769–4818).

Although San Francisco is a compact city with the prevailing influences of some neighborhoods spilling into others, the following generalizations should help you find the kind of entertainment you're looking for. **Nob Hill** is noted for its plush piano bars and panoramic skyline lounges. **North Beach**, infamous for its topless and bottomless bistros, also maintains a sense of its beatnik past and this legacy lives on in atmospheric bars and coffeehouses. **Fisherman's Wharf**, while touristy, is great for people-watching and provides plenty of impromptu entertainment from street performers. **Union Street** is home away from home for singles in search of company. **South of Market** (SoMa, for short) has become a hub of nightlife, with a bevy of highly popular nightclubs, bars, and lounges in renovated warehouses and auto shops. Gay men will find the **Castro** and **Polk Street** scenes of infinite variety.

Rock, Pop, Folk, and Blues

DNA Lounge. Mainly rock is featured, but country and jazz groups occasionally play here, too. Representative of DNA's bands are Beatnik Beach and the Sea Hags. *375 11th St. near Harrison St., tel. 415/626-1409. Live bands most nights at 10 PM. Other nights the club is open for dancing to recorded music. Cover: weeknights $3, Fri.-Sat. $7. No credit cards.*

Freight and Salvage Coffee House. This is one of the finest folk houses in the country; it's worth a trip across the bay. Some of the most talented practitioners of folk, blues, Cajun, and bluegrass perform at the Freight, among them U. Utah Phillips and Rosalie Sorrels. *1111 Addison St., Berkeley, tel. 510/548-1761. Shows: weeknights 8 PM, Fri. and Sat. 8:30. Cover: $6-$10. No credit cards.*

Great American Music Hall. This is one of the great eclectic nightclubs, not only in San Francisco but in the entire country. Here you will find truly top-drawer entertainment, running the gamut from the best in blues, folk, and jazz to rock with a sprinkling of outstanding comedians. This colorful marble-pillared emporium will also accommodate dancing to popular bands. Past headliners here include Carmen McCrae, B.B. King, Tom Paxton, and Doc Watson. *859 O'Farrell St. between Polk and Larkin Sts., tel. 415/885-0750. Shows usually at 8 PM,* *but this may vary, so call. Cover: $5–$20. No credit cards.*

I-Beam. One of the most popular of San Francisco's rock dance clubs, the I-Beam features new-wave bands and high-energy rock 'n' roll in a spacious setting. Spectacular lights and lasers enhance your dancing pleasure here. *1748 Haight St., tel. 415/668–6006. Open nightly 9 PM. Cover: $5–$10; occasionally free. No credit cards.*

Last Day Saloon. In an attractive setting of wooden tables and potted plants, this club offers some major entertainers and a varied schedule of blues, Cajun, rock, and jazz. Some of the illustrious performers who have appeared here are Taj Mahal, the Zazu Pitts Memorial Orchestra, Maria Muldaur, and Pride and Joy. *406 Clement St. between 5th and 6th Aves. in the Richmond District, tel. 415/387–6343. Shows 9 PM nightly. Cover: $4–$20. No credit cards.*

Lou's Pier 47. This Wharf restaurant features cool music and hot food on the waterfront. *300 Jefferson St., Fisherman's Wharf, tel. 414/771–0377. Afternoon and evening shows, usually 4 PM and 9 PM and Sunday afternoons at 4. Cover $4–$6 in evening. AE, MC, V.*

Paradise Lounge. This quirky lounge has three stages for eclectic live music and dancing, plus an upstairs cabaret featuring offbeat performers. *1501 Folsom St. tel. 415/861–6906. Live music 10 PM nightly. Cover: $3 Thurs. and Fri., $5 Sat. and Sun. No credit cards.*

Pier 23. This funky waterfront restaurant turns into a packed nightclub at night with a musical spectrum ranging from Caribbean, salsa, and jazz to Cajun zydeco, which has become popular in San Francisco in recent years. Get here early in the evening for dinner and you can keep your table after the music starts. *At Embarcadero and Pier 23, across from Fog City Diner. tel. 415/362-5125. Shows 9:30 PM Wed.–Sat. Cover: $5 Fri. and Sat. MC, V.*

Slim's. One of the most popular nightclubs on the SoMa scene, Slim's specializes in what it labels "American roots music"—blues, jazz, classic rock, and the like. Co-owner Boz Scaggs helps bring in the crowds and famous headliners. *333 11th St., tel. 415/621–3330. Shows nightly 9 PM. Cover $10–$20. AE, MC, V.*

The Saloon. Some locals consider the historic Saloon the best spot in San Francisco for the blues. Headliners here include local blues favorite Roy Rogers. *1232 Grant St. near Columbus Ave. in North Beach, tel. 415/989-7666. Shows 9:30 PM nightly. Cover: $5-$8 Fri. and Sat. No credit cards.*

The Stone. This club features primarily rock groups, with occasional jazz and blues performers. *412 Broadway in North Beach, tel. 415/547-1954. Shows Wed.-Sun., 8 PM. Cover: $6-$10, 2-drink minimum. No credit cards.*

The Warfield. This old Art Deco theater was completely renovated in 1988 to become a showcase for mainstream rock 'n' roll. There are tables and chairs downstairs, and theater seating upstairs. Such contemporary acts as Robert Palmer, Simply Red, and k.d. lang have played here recently. *982 Market St. tel. 415/775-7722. Shows most nights at 8 PM. Tickets $15-$20. V.*

Jazz

Jazz at Pearl's. This club is one of the few reminders of North Beach's days as a hot jazz nightspot. Sophisticated and romantic, the club's picture windows look over City Lights Bookstore across the street. *256 Columbus Ave. near Broadway. tel. 415/291-8255. Live music Tues.-Sat. at 9:30 PM. Cover: $5 on weekends.*

Kimball's East. This three-year-old club in a new shopping complex in Emeryville, just off Highway 80 near Oakland, hosts jazz greats such as Dizzy Gillespie and popular vocalists such as Lou Rawls and Patti Austin. With an elegant interior and fine food, this is one of most luxurious supper clubs in the Bay Area. *5800 Shellmound St., Emeryville, tel. 510/658-2555. Shows Fri. and Sat. at 9 and 11, Wed. and Thurs. at 8 and 10. Sun. brunch with live performances by local jazz groups, 11-2. Cover: $12-$24 with $5 minimum. $5 cover for Sun. brunch. Advance ticket purchase advised for big-name shows. MC, V.*

Pasand Lounge. Jazz and rhythm and blues are the main attractions here. *1875 Union St., Pacific Heights, tel. 415/922-4498. Shows nightly, 7 PM-1 AM. No cover. 2-drink minimum. AE, MC, V.*

Yoshi's. Although located in Oakland, Yoshi's is

well worth the trip over to the East Bay because it features some of the biggest names in jazz. The likes of Carmen McCrae, Dizzy Gillespie, and Cecil Taylor have played in this pleasant club with excellent acoustics. There is a Japanese restaurant adjacent. *6030 Claremont St. in north Oakland, just over the Berkeley line, tel. 510/652-9200. Shows weeknights at 8 and 10, Fri. and Sat. at 9 and 11. Cover: $5-$18. AE, MC, V.*

Cabarets

Club Fugazi. *Beach Blanket Babylon Goes around the World* is a wacky musical revue that has become the longest running show of its genre in the history of the theater. It has run now for well over a decade, outstripping the Ziegfeld Follies by years. While the choreography is colorful and the songs witty, the real stars of the show are the exotic costumes—worth the price of admission in themselves. Order tickets as far in advance as possible; the revue has been sold out up to a month in advance. *678 Green St., 94133, tel. 415/421-4222. Shows 8 PM Wed.-Thurs., 8 and 10:30 PM Fri.-Sat., 3 and 7:30 PM Sun. Cover: $17-$40, depending upon date and seating location. Note: those under 21 are admitted only to the Sun. matinee performance. MC, V.*

Finocchio's. Are you ready for the truly outrageous? You will redefine "queen" once you see Finocchio's female impersonators—among the finest on the planet. Finocchio's has been generating general confusion for 50 years. *506 Broadway, North Beach, tel. 415/982-9388. Note: those under 21 not admitted. Shows nightly at 8:30, 10, and 11:30, closed Mon. and Wed. Cover: $15. MC, V.*

Josie's Cabaret and Juice Joint. This small stylish café and cabaret in the predominantly gay Castro District books performers who reflect the countercultural feel of the neighborhood. *3583 16th St., at Market St., tel. 415/861-7933. Shows nightly, times vary. Cover: $6-$10. No credit cards.*

Comedy Clubs

Cobb's Comedy Club. Bobby Slayton, Paula Poundstone, and Dr. Gonzo are among the super stand-up comics who perform here. *In the Cannery, 2801 Leavenworth St. at the corner of Beach St., tel. 415/928-4320. Shows Mon. 8 PM, Tues.-Thurs. 9 PM, Fri.-Sat. 9 and 11 PM. Cover: $8 weeknights, $10 and 2-drink minimum Fri. and Sat. MC, V.*

Holy City Zoo. Robin Williams ascended like a meteor from an improv group that gained fame here, and terrific stand-up comics, such as local favorite Michael Prichard, headline now. The "Zoo" features comedy nightly, with an open mike for pros and would-be comedians every Tuesday. *408 Clement St. in the Richmond District, tel. 415/386-4242. Shows Sun.-Thurs. 9 PM, Fri.-Sat. 9 and 11 PM. Cover: $3 Sun.-Thurs., $8 Fri. and Sat., 2-drink minimum. MC, V.*

The Punch Line. A launching pad for the likes of Jay Leno and Whoopie Goldberg, the Punch Line features some of the top talents around—several of whom are certain to make a national impact. Note that weekend shows often sell out, and it is best to buy tickets in advance at BASS outlets (tel. 415/762-BASS). *444-A Battery St. between Clay and Washington Sts., tel. 415/397-PLSF. Shows Sun.-Thurs. 9 PM, Fri. 9 and 11 PM, Sat. 7, 9, and 11:30 PM. Cover: $8 Tues.-Thurs.; $10 Fri. and Sat.; special $5 showcases Mon. and Sun. 2-drink minimum. MC, V.*

Dancing Emporiums

Cesar's Palace. Salsa-style Latin music attracts all kinds of dancers to this popular club in the city's Hispanic Mission District. Note: no alcohol is served here. *3140 Mission St., tel. 415/648-6611. Open Fri.-Sun. 9 PM-5 AM. Cover: $7.*

Club DV8. One of the largest of the trendy SoMa clubs, DV8 attracts scores of stylish young people to its 25,000 square feet (two levels) of dance floors. *540 Howard St., tel. 415/957-1730. Open Wed.-Sat. 9 PM-3 AM. Cover: $5-$10.*

Club O. This dance spot gets its name from the swimming pool adjacent. It was the original

SoMa crossover bar. The cover charge varies. Note: You must be 21 to enter. *278 11th St., South of Market, tel. 415/621–8119. Opens 9:30 PM.*

Oz. The most popular upscale disco in San Francisco, the land of Oz is reached via a glass elevator. Then, surrounded by a splendid panorama of the city, you dance on marble floors and recharge on cushy sofas and bamboo chairs. The fine sound system belts out oldies, disco, Motown, and new wave. *335 Powell St. between Geary and Post Sts. on the top floor of the Westin St. Francis Hotel, tel. 415/397–7000. Open nightly 9 PM–2 AM. Cover: $8 Sun.–Thurs.; $15 Fri.–Sat.*

The Kennel Club. Alternative rock and funk rule in this small, steamy room: Everyone's dancing! On Thursdays and Saturdays this space is known as The Box, and a very gay mixed-gender, mixed-race crowd takes over. *628 Divisadero, tel. 415/931–1914. Open nightly 9 PM–2 AM. Cover: $2–$10.*

Piano Bars

Act IV Lounge. A popular spot for a romantic rendezvous, the focal point of this elegant lounge is a crackling fireplace. *At the Inn of the Opera, 333 Fulton St. near Franklin St., tel. 415/863–8400. Pianist nightly 6–9. No cover.*

Club 36. Relax to piano music or jazz combos while enjoying the view from the top floor of the newly renovated Grand Hyatt at Union Square. *345 Stockton St., tel. 415/398–1234. Piano or jazz nightly 5:30–7:30 PM, 9 PM–1 AM. No cover.*

Redwood Room. You will find an easy-listening atmosphere here in this sumptuous Art Deco setting. *In the Clift Hotel, Taylor and Geary Sts., tel. 415/775–4700. No cover. Dress: formal.*

Washington Square Bar and Grill. A favorite of San Francisco politicians and newspapermen, the "Washbag," as it is affectionately known, hosts pianists performing jazz and popular standards. *On North Beach's Washington Square, 1707 Powell St., tel. 415/982–8123. Music Mon.–Sat. from 9 PM. No cover.*

Skyline Bars

Carnelian Room. At 781 feet above the ground, enjoy dinner or cocktails here on the 52nd floor, where you may drink from the loftiest view of San Francisco's magnificent skyline. Reservations are a must for dinner here. *Top of the Bank of America Building, 555 California St., tel. 415/433–7500. Open Mon.–Thurs. 3 PM–midnight, Fri. 3 PM–1 AM, Sat. 4 PM–1 AM, Sunday 10 AM–midnight.*

Cityscape. At the top of the Hilton's tower, a live band plays rock, pop, and jazz for dancing beneath the stars. *In the Hilton Hotel, Mason and O'Farrell Sts., tel. 415/771–1400. Open nightly 5 PM–1 AM. No cover.*

Crown Room. Just ascending to the well-named Crown Room is a drama in itself as you take the Fairmont's glass-enclosed Skylift elevator to the top. Some San Franciscans maintain that this lounge is the most luxurious of the city's skyline bars. Lunches, dinners, and Sunday brunches are served as well as drinks. *29th floor of the Fairmont Hotel, California and Mason Sts., tel. 415/772–5131. Open daily 11 AM–1 AM.*

Equinox. What's distinctive about the Hyatt Regency's skyline-view bar is its capacity to revolve atop its 22nd floor perch, offering 360-degree views to guests from their seats. *At the Hyatt Regency, 5 Embarcadero Center, tel. 415/788–1234. Open Mon.–Sat. 11 AM–2:30 PM and 6 PM–1:30 AM, Sun. 11 AM–3:30 PM.*

Phineas T. Barnacle. This bar offers a unique panorama with views not of rooftops but of seal rocks and the horizon of the great Pacific Ocean. *In the Cliff House, 1090 Point Lobos Ave., tel. 415/386–7630. Open Mon.–Sat. 11 AM–2 AM, Sun. 10AM–2 AM.*

Starlite Roof. In this 21st-story glassed-in lounge, you may dance to a band playing primarily '50s and '60s hits. *In the Sir Francis Drake Hotel, Powell and Sutter Sts., tel. 415/392–7755. Open daily 4:30 PM–1:30 AM. No cover.*

Top of the Mark. This fabled landmark affords fabulous views in an elegant 19th-floor setting. *In the Mark Hopkins Hotel, California and Mason Sts., tel. 415/392–3434. Open nightly 4 PM–1:30 AM.*

View Lounge. Found on the 39th floor of the San

Francisco Marriott, one of the newest and loveliest of the city's skyline lounges features live piano music. *777 Market St., tel. 415/896-1600. Open noon-2 AM daily.*

Singles Bars

Balboa Cafe. A jam-packed hang-out for the young, upwardly mobile crowd, this bar/restaurant is famous for its burgers and single clientele. *3199 Fillmore St., tel. 415/921-3944. Open nightly until 2 AM.*

Hard Rock Cafe. Part of the famous chain of youth-oriented bars, this crowded saloon is filled with a collection of rock 'n' roll memorabilia that won't disappoint Hard Rock fans. *1699 Van Ness Ave., tel. 415/885-1699. Open Sun.-Thurs. until 12:30 AM, Fri.-Sat. until 1 AM.*

Harrington's. This Irish drinking saloon is the place to be on St. Patrick's Day. *245 Front St., tel. 415/392-7595. Open Mon. and Tues. 9 AM-10 PM; Wed. and Thurs. 9 AM-11 PM; Fri. 9 AM-midnight; Sat. 11 AM-7 PM. Closed Sun.*

Harry Denton's. The liveliest, trendiest, most upscale saloon to open in San Francisco in years, Denton's is packed with well-dressed young professionals. It's location on the Embarcadero, where the freeway recently came down, affords stunning views of the bay from the back bar. *161 Steuart St., tel. 415/882-1333. Open Wed.-Thurs. 11:30-11 PM, Fri.-Sat. until midnight. Dancing after 10 PM.*

The Holding Company. This is one of the most popular weeknight Financial District watering holes, where scores of office workers gather to enjoy friendly libations. *In 2 Embarcadero Center, tel. 415/986-0797. Open Mon.-Tues. until midnight, Wed.-Fri. until 2 AM. Closed weekends.*

Perry's. Usually jam-packed, Perry's is the most famous of San Francisco's singles bars. You can dine here on great hamburgers as well as more substantial fare. *1944 Union St. at Buchanan St., tel. 415/922-9022. Open daily 9 AM-2 AM.*

San Francisco's Favorite Bars

Buena Vista. Even though the Buena Vista's claim of having introduced Irish Coffee to the New World may be dubious, this is the Wharf area's most popular bar. Usually packed with tourists, it has a fine view of the waterfront. *2765 Hyde St. near Fisherman's Wharf, tel. 415/ 474-5044.*

Edinburgh Castle. This is a delightful Scottish drinking emporium, with a jukebox that breathes Scottish airs and live bagpipes on weekends. The decor is Scottish, the bartender is Scottish, and there are plenty of Scottish brews from which to choose. You can work off the fish-and-chips variety fare with a turn at the dart board. *950 Geary St. near Polk St., tel. 415/ 885-4074.*

House of Shields. For a taste of an authentic old-time San Francisco saloon, try this bar, which attracts an older, Financial District crowd after work. It closes at 8 PM. *39 New Montgomery St., tel. 415/392-7732.*

John's Grill. Located on the fringe of the Tenderloin, this bar was featured in The Maltese Falcon and mystery fans will revel in its Hammett memorabilia. *63 Ellis St., tel. 415/986-0069.*

Peer Inn. If you want to get away from the tourist scene while at the waterfront, this is a good place in which to imbibe. Peer Inn has an adjacent restaurant. *Pier 33 at the Embarcadero at the end of Bay St., tel. 415/788-1411.*

Spec's. It's worth looking for this somewhat hard-to-find hangout for artists, poets, and seamen. Spec's is a wonderful watering hole hideaway, reflecting a sense of the North Beach of days gone by. *12 Adler Place near the intersection of Broadway and Columbus Ave., tel. 415/ 421-4112.*

Tosca Café. Like Spec's and Vesuvio nearby, Tosca holds a special place in San Francisco lore. There is some Italian flavor, with opera and Italian standards on the jukebox and an antique espresso/cappuccino machine that is nothing less than a work of art. Known as a hang-out for filmmaker Francis Ford Coppola, whose office is nearby, playwright/actor Sam Shepard, and ballet star Mikhail Barishnikov (when they're in town), this place positively breathes a film noir atmosphere. *At 242 Columbus. tel. 415/391-1244.*

Vesuvio Cafe. Near the legendary City Lights Bookstore, this quintessentially North Beach bar is little altered since its heyday as a haven for the Beat poets. *255 Columbus Ave. between Broadway and Pacific Ave., tel. 415/362–3370.*

Gay Bars

Kimo's. This relaxed establishment affords an elegant ambience. *1351 Polk St., tel. 415/885–4535.*

The Midnight Sun. This is one of the Castro's longest-standing and most popular bars, with giant video screens riotously programmed. *4067 18th St., tel. 415/861–4186.*

The Stud. This is a popular, jam-packed SoMa bar. *399 9th St., tel. 415/863–6623.*

Twin Peaks. A pleasant mirrored fern bar, Twin Peaks is a tranquil place in which to drink and converse. *401 Castro St., tel. 415/864–9470.*

Index

Fodor's Travel Guides

U.S. Guides

Alaska

Arizona

Boston

California

Cape Cod, Martha's
Vineyard, Nantucket

The Carolinas & the
Georgia Coast

Chicago

Disney World & the
Orlando Area

Florida

Hawaii

Las Vegas, Reno,
Tahoe

Los Angeles

Maine, Vermont,
New Hampshire

Maui

Miami & the Keys

New England

New Orleans

New York City

Pacific North Coast

Philadelphia & the
Pennsylvania Dutch
Country

San Diego

San Francisco

Santa Fe, Taos,
Albuquerque

Seattle & Vancouver

The South

The U.S. & British
Virgin Islands

The Upper Great
Lakes Region

USA

Vacations in New York
State

Vacations on the
Jersey Shore

Virginia & Maryland

Waikiki

Washington, D.C.

Foreign Guides

Acapulco, Ixtapa,
Zihuatanejo

Australia & New
Zealand

Austria

The Bahamas

Baja & Mexico's
Pacific Coast Resorts

Barbados

Berlin

Bermuda

Brazil

Budapest

Budget Europe

Canada

Cancun, Cozumel,
Yucatan Peninsula

Caribbean

Central America

China

Costa Rica, Belize,
Guatemala

Czechoslovakia

Eastern Europe

Egypt

Euro Disney

Europe

Europe's Great Cities

France

Germany

Great Britain

Greece

The Himalayan
Countries

Hong Kong

India

Ireland

Israel

Italy

Italy's Great Cities

Japan

Kenya & Tanzania

Korea

London

Madrid & Barcelona

Mexico

Montreal &
Quebec City

Morocco

The Netherlands
Belgium &
Luxembourg

New Zealand

Norway

Nova Scotia, Prince
Edward Island &
New Brunswick

Paris

Portugal

Rome

Russia & the Baltic
Countries

Scandinavia

Scotland

Singapore

South America

Southeast Asia

South Pacific

Spain

Sweden

Switzerland

Thailand

Tokyo

Toronto

Turkey

Vienna & the Danube
Valley

Yugoslavia

WHEREVER YOU TRAVEL, *H*ELP IS NEVER FAR AWAY.

From planning your trip to replacing
lost Cards, American Express® Travel Service
Offices* are always there to help.

SAN FRANCISCO
237 Post St.
415-981-5533

455 Market St.
415-512-8250

295 California St.
415-788-4367

Sheraton
Fisherman's Wharf
2500 Mason Street
415-788-3025

CARMEL
Bob McGinnis Travel, Inc.
561 Carmel Rancho
Shopping Center
408-624-2724

NAPA
Thompson Travel
3308 Jefferson St.
707-255-8737

OAKLAND
500 12th St., Suite 115
510-834-2833

PALO ALTO
393 Stanford Shopping Center
415-327-3711

SAN RAFAEL
Terra Linda Travel
515 Northgate Dr.
415-492-0333

WALNUT CREEK
Broadway Plaza
91 Broadway Lane
510-938-0800